The

1999 Guide
to Feng Shui and
Chinese Astrology

D1189940

Rocky Sung is a respected authority on Feng Shui, highly commendable for his honesty, directness and professionalism. He studies all factors involved and considers all available resources before making any recommendations. He does not propose major changes that will waste current resources, but rather suggests improvements that will maximize their full Feng Shui potential. His expertise and improvements have induced a more positive relationship between man and his environment.

Andre G Rolli, General Manager,
Westin Hotel, Shanghai

The

1999 Guide
to Feng Shui and
Chinese Astrology

Rocky Siu-Kwong Sung

edited by Teresa Franklin

Thorsons
An Imprint of HarperCollins*Publishers*

Thorsons
An Imprint of HarperCollins*Publishers*
77–85 Fulham Palace Road
Hammersmith, London W6 8JB

Published by Thorsons 1998
3 5 7 9 10 8 6 4 2

A catalogue record for this book
is available from the British Library

ISBN 0 7225 3725 5

Phototypeset by Harper Phototypesetters Limited,
Northampton, England
Printed and bound in Great Britain by
Caledonian International Book Manufacturing Ltd, Glasgow

Contents

About the Author

Sung Siu-Kwong, hereafter referred to as Rocky Sung, is instantly recognizable by the international Chinese community as the top Feng Shui Master of what must surely be the Feng Shui capital of the world – Hong Kong.

His many best-selling Chinese books on Feng Shui, a successful Feng Shui television programme viewed by Chinese communities across the globe, countless interviews on international television shows such as CNN, press and magazine interviews conducted in many languages, plus his reputation as a scrupulous results-driven consultant have assured him this international recognition.

Born in China, Sung grew up in Hong Kong. He graduated from Taiwan University with a degree in history, and went on to obtain his Master's Degree from the University of Illinois. His interest in Feng Shui dates back to his school days, when his love of hiking found him out on the rigorous mountain trails of the territory. It was on these outdoor expeditions that an elderly master taught him how to locate the 'veins of the dragon', or the flow of the mountain. As his knowledge of Chinese history grew, so too did his knowledge of this ancient Chinese tradition.

Sung has millions of followers and an enviable multinational blue-chip client list which includes the prestigious retail chain

Marks & Spencer, the Swire Group of Companies and the Westin International Hotel Group.

Westerners in Hong Kong have long followed the beliefs of their Chinese counterparts; now, as the entire Western world expresses an interest in Eastern philosophies and traditions, the name Rocky Sung has become increasingly synonymous with the art of Feng Shui throughout the world.

He has offices in Hong Kong and Los Angeles, and family contacts in New York.

Introduction

This book is unique and outstanding because it consists of the following four key factors that distinguish it from all the other books about Chinese Horoscope:

1 The application of the traditional Stars in the Chinese Horoscope into the calculation of the fate of different Signs.
2 The use of proverbs to indicate the fate of a Sign for a particular month.
3 The application of Feng Shui to improve the fortune of different Signs.
4 An easy-to-read chart to remind readers of how to 'do the right things at the right time every day' in 1999 (the Day-by-day Analysis of Luck).

Application of Traditional Stars of the Chinese Horoscope

This is the first book in English which uses a pure Chinese Horoscope methodology to predict the future. It is not at all influenced by Western Astrology. Chinese traditional Astrology is completely different to Western Astrology.

The Chinese method of predicting the future was developed some 2,000 years ago, and calculated according to the distribution of Stars within a specific Sign. The number of Lucky and Unlucky Stars within a Sign determines a person's fate for the year. Obviously this distribution of Stars varies on a year-to-year basis for each Star, therefore the fate of each Sign changes annually.

This calculating system has been practised in China for centuries and has proved to be quite effective. I have applied this system in the writing of my Chinese-language yearly fortune book, which has sold in large numbers, since 1985.

The Lucky and Unlucky Stars of the Chinese Horoscope have a very long history. Given the history of Chinese predictions and the usage of these Stars, to attempt to forecast the future without applying the traditional method, as is so often seen in Western books on Chinese Astrology, is definitely incorrect. Unfortunately a lot of so-called 'Chinese Horoscope' books in print are therefore inaccurate.

I have no bias towards Western or Indian Astrology – quite the contrary, I have a deep and sincere respect for them. However, a mixture of Chinese and Western Astrology seems awkward, and the substance of the work is very much diminished by trying to mix the two. It destroys the basic nature of each method.

Considering that most non-Chinese readers have no knowledge of the Stars which influence the Chinese Astrological predictions, I have explained the origins, meaning and modern implication of each one (see pages 194–213). After reading the Stars, both Lucky and Unlucky, which apply to their Sign for the forthcoming year, readers will have a clear picture of their fate.

This book provides the reader with predictions for the entire year, with daily reference charts for every day of the year in the Chinese Calendar (see pages 110–93).

The monthly prognosis is to prepare the reader on how to face each month. It will give you the opportunity to protect yourself when facing bad luck, and it will give you the opportunity to activate initiatives when you know you are heading for good luck.

The 12 Chinese Horoscope Signs

The Mouse (Rat)
The Ox
The Tiger
The Rabbit
The Dragon
The Snake
The Horse
The Sheep (Goat)
The Monkey
The Rooster
The Dog
The Pig

Individuals are classified according to their birth date. The chart on page xv will allow readers to check which is their Sign.

SNAKE	HORSE	SHEEP	MONKEY
DRAGON			ROOSTER
RABBIT			DOG
TIGER	OX	MOUSE	PIG

Figure 1

The 12 Signs are divided into 12 squares as shown in Figure 1. The distribution of the Stars, both Lucky and Unlucky, will determine the fate of each of the 12 Signs for the year.

The Stars are not evenly distributed; this makes a difference. Each Star is listed individually so that the reader has a clear picture of his or her fortune. Those Signs with more Lucky Stars will have a good year, while those with more Unlucky Stars will have a rough, even a poor, year. There are 21 Lucky Stars and 47 Unlucky Stars mentioned in this book.

Proverbs and Fortune

Each chapter for a particular Sign has a General Overview of the Year for 1999, followed by Monthly In-depth Forecasts. Each of these monthly sections begins with a proverb, to enable readers to know at a glance precisely what challenges they are going to face in a given month.

Proverbs are derived from the experiences of daily life. Therefore, after very careful consideration I have decided upon an appropriate proverb to summarize the monthly fortune for each Sign. Through this I hope that readers will have a much better understanding of their fortune for each month.

I sincerely hope that this method of my own will benefit readers throughout the world.

Using Feng Shui

The main Feng Shui tactics are discussed in a chapter of their own at the end of this book. Each outlines the Feng Shui directions, colour, lucky numbers and lucky charms for each Sign.

These Feng Shui tactics are practical and effective in improving the fortune of every Sign. They are based on the calculation of the Five Elements, the Yin and Yang and the distribution of Lucky and Unlucky Stars throughout the year.

Just as different kinds of medicine will suit different people, different Feng Shui tactics will suit different Signs. To avoid taking the wrong 'medicine', readers should therefore not try to apply the Feng Shui recommended for any Sign but their own.

Day-by-day Analysis of Luck

From the experiences of their daily lives through numerous generations, the ancient Chinese found that certain activities would meet with much greater success if undertaken on certain days. Along the same line, certain things can go wrong if attempted on the wrong day. Thus the ancient Chinese realized that there was a close correlation between human activities and certain days.

Consequently, the concept of 'doing the right thing at the right time every day' has been deeply ingrained into the Chinese psyche and society for centuries.

The Day-by-day Analysis of Luck table will prove helpful in improving one's overall fortune. The same charts have appeared in my Chinese-language books, and have been proven useful to my readers over the past 13 years.

How to Establish Your Chinese Sign

1901 --- Ox	1902 --- Tiger **	1903 --- Rabbit **	1904 --- Dragon **
1905 --- Snake	1906 --- Horse **	1907 --- Sheep **	1908 --- Monkey **
1909 ---Rooster	1910 --- Dog **	1911 --- Pig **	1912 --- Mouse **
1913 --- Ox	1914 --- Tiger	1915 --- Rabbit **	1916 --- Dragon **
1917 --- Snake	1918 --- Horse	1919 --- Sheep **	1920 --- Monkey **
1921 --- Rooster	1922 --- Dog	1923 --- Pig **	1924 --- Mouse **
1925 --- Ox	1926 --- Tiger	1927 --- Rabbit **	1928 --- Dragon **
1929 --- Snake	1930 --- Horse	1931 --- Sheep **	1932 --- Monkey **
1933 --- Rooster	1934 --- Dog	1935 --- Pig **	1936 --- Mouse **
1937 --- Ox	1938 --- Tiger	1939 --- Rabbit **	1940 --- Dragon **
1941 --- Snake	1942 --- Horse	1943 --- Sheep **	1944 --- Monkey **
1945 --- Rooster	1946 --- Dog	1947 --- Pig	1948 --- Mouse **
1949 --- Ox	1950 --- Tiger	1951 --- Rabbit	1952 --- Dragon **
1953 --- Snake	1954 --- Horse	1955 --- Sheep	1956 --- Monkey **
1957 --- Rooster	1958 --- Dog	1959 --- Pig	1960 --- Mouse **
1961 --- Ox	1962 --- Tiger	1963 --- Rabbit	1964 --- Dragon **
1965 --- Snake	1966 --- Horse	1967 --- Sheep	1968 --- Monkey **
1969 --- Rooster	1970 --- Dog	1971 --- Pig	1972 --- Mouse **
1973 --- Ox	1974 --- Tiger	1975 --- Rabbit	1976 --- Dragon **
1977 --- Snake	1978 --- Horse	1979 --- Sheep	1980 --- Monkey **
1981 --- Rooster	1982 --- Dog	1983 --- Pig	1984 --- Mouse
1985 --- Ox	1986 --- Tiger	1987 --- Rabbit	1988 --- Dragon
1989 --- Snake	1990 --- Horse	1991 --- Sheep	1992 --- Monkey
1993 --- Rooster	1994 --- Dog	1995 --- Pig	1996 --- Mouse
1997 --- Ox	1998 --- Tiger	1999 --- Rabbit	2000 --- Dragon

According to the Chinese Horoscope, people are classified into a certain Sign according to their birth year. This chart will help you to establish your exact Sign.

There is a difference between the Chinese calendar and the Western calendar. The secret is that 4th February of the Western calendar is the dividing line. For example, if a person was born on 3rd February 1998, then he is considered to be an Ox. But if he was born on 5th February 1998, then he is considered to be a Tiger.

Occasionally this dividing line changes to 5th February. This will mean a slight adjustment. These exceptional years are indicated on this chart by **.

Chapter One

鼠

The

Mouse (Rat)

Years of the Mouse

Please keep in mind when consulting the list below that the Chinese New Year begins in early February – for example, in 1960 'the year of the Mouse' covers the period 5th February 1960 to 3rd February 1961.

1912	1960
1924	1972
1936	1984
1948	1996

Distribution of the Stars within the Sign for 1999

Lucky Stars	Unlucky Stars
Pink Phoenix	Pool of Indulgence
Star of Blessing	Tongues Wag
Heavenly Virtue	Funeral Robe
Blessing Virtue	

Please refer to pages 194–213 for traditional Chinese origins of and meanings for these Stars.

General Overview of the Year

The indications are that 1999 will be a very fortunate year for the Mouse. You can expect to execute all your responsibilities smoothly and with the backing of very important and influential people. Your relationships will be good, and this year promises to be filled with romance. However, don't abuse this good luck. The Mouse may have a tendency to indulge in many love affairs and other bad habits – this must be avoided.

The start of the year is particularly good and it is possible that the Mouse may find a suitable companion within the first two months. You should keep away from alcohol and drugs.

The fate of the Mouse will change from good to bad during the month of the Rabbit. Look after the health of elderly family members, spend time with them, before it is too late.

The month of the Dragon will be very busy in both business and social aspects. This active involvement will result in just rewards. There will be considerable returns on financial investments, and there could be an unexpected windfall.

Bad luck will come as suddenly in the month of the Snake as a summer thunderstorm, without any warning. The Mouse will be involved in disputes and conflict. Try to remain neutral and calm, and avoid the controversy.

The months of the Monkey and Rooster will be the most fortunate period of the year. Make the most of this period of opportunity in order to secure an important breakthrough at the end of the year. You will get a promotion with help from a very influential person. You will also enjoy a sweet family life if you get married within this period.

A downward trend is expected in the months of the Rooster and Dog. It is advisable for the Mouse to make a concentrated effort to stop the constant indulgence in bad habits or you could end up in deep trouble. Also avoid gossiping and be nice to friends and colleagues.

The year ends as it began, on a high note. During the months of the Pig, Mouse and Ox, the Mouse will once again enjoy a harmonious relationship with associates, friends and family. There could be an important breakthrough in career or academia particularly, if you have applied yourself throughout the year. The income of the Mouse will be increased substantially.

Monthly In-depth Forecasts
Tiger Month (16th February – 17th March)

Eagles don't catch flies

This year will begin well for the Mouse. You will set your sights high and have tremendous energy and drive to face all challenges. There could be an important breakthrough in your career, however you should be careful not to be distracted from goals, focusing only on the important issues and delegating smaller tasks, or you could miss many good opportunities.

Remember, 'big eagles will only catch bigger prey.'

This is indeed a good month for the Mouse. Apart from a rise up the career ladder, indications are that monetary income will be good, and there is a considerable chance of winning a handsome prize. Be careful regarding the outflow of capital or you may find yourself over-extended.

This will also be a romantic month for the Mouse. There will be an opportunity to meet your dream lover. A word of caution: proceed slowly or this opportunity for true love could be ruined before it starts.

Rabbit Month (18th March – 15th April)

Hope for the best, prepare for the worst

The Mouse will begin to feel a gentle downward trend. There will be some opposition and some challenges, which will cause stress and take a lot of time and energy to handle. The best advice is to 'slow down a little'; you need to think, and a hasty decision could lead to a fall.

The Mouse should be alert and prepare for the worst, as this period promises to be very difficult. Don't risk any money gambling or in big investments. Be very careful to protect personal belongings and beware of pick-pockets.

Dragon Month (16th April – 14th May)

Appearances can be deceptive

It is important for the Mouse to be alert or you could be easily misled. Remember 'seeing is *not* believing' and wolves will hide behind a friendly and sincere mask. Before entering into any legal agreement or contract, make sure you read the fine print – even better, seek professional help from a solicitor to avoid costly mistakes.

The health of the Mouse is very stable right now. Elderly members of the family may need some special care right now; make sure you give them the attention they need, or it could be too late.

Snake Month (15th May – 13th June)

Walls have ears

There is a slightly bumpy road ahead, but all obstacles will gradually be overcome as things begin once more to improve for the Mouse. Keep a low profile. This is not the time to indulge in office gossip – the wrong person may overhear, and you could suffer the consequences.

Finances are good. Expect a good return on investments, plus an unexpected windfall. Any loan applications will be approved. Don't, however, invest in property for the time being.

Horse Month (14th June – 12th July)

Time and tide wait for no man

The Mouse could be presented with many career opportunities – be wise and choose with care. You should not wait too long before making your decision, as these chances will slip through your fingers should you procrastinate. A wise and speedy decision is called for.

The health of the Mouse will improve greatly during this period. However, 'water' will present a big threat to you, so take special care should you be taken on a fishing trip, or when swimming.

The Mouse could experience some jealousy. You should conduct yourself in an exemplary fashion. Don't try to trick or fool anyone, or it could backfire. Socially the Mouse is encouraged to be friendly, approachable and amiable – this kind of personable behaviour will be handsomely rewarded.

Sheep Month (13th July – 10th August)

Bad money drives out good

The Mouse will face strong challenges during this period, and you will need to do your best to handle this situation or you could end up forfeiting everything. There will be some serious disagreement at work. It is advisable to gain the support of colleagues or risk the possibility of being driven out like 'good money driven out by bad'.

The Mouse will have a pretty good income, but unfortunately it will not be easy to hold on to. The money will disappear without any warning if you don't keep a close eye on it. Definitely do not enter into a loan arrangement with a friend as the money is likely to be lost along with the friendship.

On the romantic front, a third party could drive a wedge between you and your loved one. Don't underestimate this stranger; he or she could seriously damage the relationship. To repeat, 'beware: bad money drives out good.'

Monkey Month (11th August – 9th September)

The harder you work the luckier you get

Business will run very smoothly this month. Your workload will be very heavy – it needs to be handled efficiently and effectively; it is critical to do it right and to do it fast. Thereafter chances will open up. The months of July and August are very important for the Mouse as it is over this period that you will reach your full working potential.

The message is clear: work very hard, capitalize on this productive period and don't let opportunities pass you by. If these opportunities are missed the rest of the year could be fruitless.

This is an excellent time for business or leisure travel. The Mouse could meet an influential person, but romance is not featured.

Rooster Month (10th September – 8th October)

Opportunity doesn't knock twice

Opportunities continue for the Mouse. Out of all these options there is one which is significant; the Mouse must be sensitive enough to recognize and choose the right one without hesitating too long. This is the chance of a lifetime.

The Mouse will get a promotion due to sheer hard work. Should you want to change jobs, this is the right time to make the move. Care should be taken to avoid arrogance in order to prevent unnecessary hostility and distrust.

The Mouse will experience a strong sexual attraction this month. This is a temporary attraction and the Mouse should not expect too much or could end up disappointed. In fact there will be no romantic breakthrough this period.

The Mouse does have a secret admirer. Whilst this is a boost to the ego, it is not someone to whom the Mouse would feel mutually attracted.

Dog Month (9th October – 7th November)

A problem shared is a problem halved

Don't be a hero by carrying the world on your shoulders; it will undoubtedly be too much for you to bear. It will be more beneficial to invite those involved to discuss and solve the problems which present themselves. It would pay the Mouse to be less repressive, and to remember that there is nothing dishonourable about sharing pain and suffering; in fact it will bring with it a feeling of relief, and certainly lighten the load.

Healthwise this is a reasonable month for the Mouse, however, extra time and care should be given to the children of the house; make sure they do not go too near water or steps. In addition the Mouse should drive carefully, especially at night.

Emotions will be running high. It appears that there will be a great deal of disagreement and conflict both at home and at the office. My advice is to walk away and gain composure; it would be advisable not to lose complete control of your emotions.

Pig Month (8th November – 7th December)

Desperate diseases must have desperate remedies

This will be the most difficult and challenging month of the year for the Mouse. Opponents will use many different strategies to gain the upper hand and dominate the Mouse. In the struggle for survival the Mouse will need to use every trick in the book, including more dramatic measures. You are not likely to win by using traditional methods.

The good fortune of the Mouse is fading. It will be necessary to secure property, as a robbery or break-in could occur at the beginning of this period.

Don't make any financial promises or deals – they could lead to trouble later. Remember: 'out of debt, out of danger.'

Mouse Month (8th December 1999 – 6th January 2000)

The sooner begun, the sooner done

With the help of an influential person, the Mouse will have an important career breakthrough mid-month. Take advantage of this opportunity immediately. A quick and early start on this offer will eliminate competitors and secure a better result. Be very careful about choosing the right partner; there are plenty of hypocrites around.

This is an excellent time to start a new project.

The fortune of the Mouse is very good until year end. Go ahead with long-term investments, such as starting a new business or buying property. Gambling should be avoided, especially at the beginning of the month.

Ox Month (7th January – 4th February 2000)

Strike while the iron is hot

There will be plenty of opportunities for the Mouse this month. Try to take advantage by using these opportunities, as you will secure success in coming years. To hesitate will be costly, so stop all the idle talk and take action, or someone else will step in and take over.

The Mouse is indeed experiencing good fortune. It is a good time to buy a car or a house. A pay rise can be expected before the end of the month. If travelling on business or holiday, take care of personal possessions, especially wallets, purses, and passports.

You and your loved one will enjoy a romantic month. Be honest with each other or there could be some unnecessary misunderstandings. Try not to indulge in bad habits, especially sexual encounters with anyone other than your partner.

Chapter Two

The

Ox

Years of the Ox

Please keep in mind when consulting the list below that the Chinese New Year begins in early February – for example, in 1961 'the year of the Ox' covers the period 4th February 1961 to 3rd February 1962.

1913	1961
1925	1973
1937	1985
1949	1997

Distribution of the Stars within the Sign for 1999

Lucky Stars	Unlucky Stars
None	Isolated Living
	Leopard's Tail
	Lunar Threat
	Funeral Guest
	Loose Hair
	Dog of Heaven

Please refer to pages 194–213 for traditional Chinese origins of and meanings for these Stars.

General Overview of the Year

The Ox faces a very difficult year in 1999, unless you are prepared to take all aspects of your life, particularly business and finance, seriously. The reason for this is the appearance of several Unlucky Stars, and no Lucky Stars to neutralize the effect. This is simply a warning to the Ox, to take some precautionary measures in advance as prevention. The correct attitude to the Chinese Horoscope is to treat it in much the same manner as fishermen would treat a stormy sea alert. It is the people with strong wills and good spirits who survive the storm best. It is almost entirely up to the fishermen.

The first two months of business will be sluggish; you will be disappointed if you have relied on last year's projects to bring in the money. You should work harder and be more co-operative with those around you.

The Dragon month and Horse month will see an upward trend financially for the Ox. Careerwise this will also be a much better period. You need to be self-sufficient as you cannot depend on other people in this period. This will need all the strength the Ox has because it will be quite a struggle. You should be quick to act if an opportunity presents itself, as there is a good chance it may slip through your fingers.

There will be yet more difficulties in love and business in the months of the Sheep and Monkey, but hang in there Ox, persevere, don't give in too early or too easily.

The Rooster month will be a most fortunate time for the Ox. Make the most of this month. It could make the struggle worth while, and make the year a productive one.

The Dog and Pig months are again problematic. The Ox must learn to keep his (or her) inquisitive nature under control. Pay attention to your own affairs and don't interfere in other people's business. Don't make comparisons or be judgemental, it will cause a lot of unnecessary trouble.

All through the year the fortune of the Ox will fluctuate, but finances are pretty good in the Mouse month. Business and finances are difficult in the month of the Ox. It is imperative that you protect rewards for which you have worked so long and so hard.

Monthly In-depth Forecasts
Tiger Month (16th February – 17th March)

There are no birds in last year's nest

The Ox will be disappointed in career advancement this month. Your expectations for continued development will not be realized, instead you will be as disturbed as a child discovering there are 'no more eggs in last year's nest'. This is a slow and somewhat troublesome phase, so besides keeping a low profile it would be advisable to perform all duties in an exemplary fashion. This attitude and behaviour will help you get through.

Finances, too, are expected to be low; there could be financial difficulties towards the end of the month if spending is not curbed.

The Ox will be surrounded by people, but there will be a sense of loneliness. It will be difficult to find someone to confide in. Affairs of the heart will be quiet and empty.

Rabbit Month (18th March – 15th April)

You can't get blood from a stone

Intelligence is called for this month, especially when it comes to making a choice. Choosing the right option will save a great deal of wasted time and energy. This is a time for developing long-term relationships with clients, not for a career change. The dark clouds overhead will disperse at the end of the month.

There is no improvement in finances this month. This presents an opportunity to become self-sufficient. Don't rely on outside help, because it is not likely to materialize – 'you can't get blood from a stone'.

The possessive streak in the Ox is likely to show itself this month. Jealousy and suspicion should be avoided. It is much wiser to stay calm and modest.

Dragon Month (16th April – 14th May)

He that would eat the fruit must climb the tree

In the third month of the year the Ox has an opportunity to climb out of the rut. This will take a lot of hard work, particularly as the Ox cannot depend on anyone for help. To eat the delicious fruit at the top of the tree one needs to climb the tree first. Choose the fruit carefully as it is easy to pick a rotten one.

The Ox is healthy this month. In the first half of the month, make sure all food is cleaned and cooked properly as there is a possibility of ingesting either bad food or taking an overdose. Keep out of water at the end of the month.

Snake Month (15th May – 13th June)

The end crowns the works

The Ox will have the energy and the guts to start a new project this month. If you desire a career change this is a good time to make it. There could be many difficulties later, but my advice is – don't give up, especially if this is a meaningful position. Endeavour to find people willing to help in future developments.

The finances of the Ox will be very good this month, there will be additional income and, if desired, a loan will be granted.

The health of the Ox is very good. You will be in peak condition both physically and mentally. If there are young children at home take care of them. Avoid alcohol.

Horse Month (14th June – 12th July)

Delays are dangerous

This is a month of strong challenges for the Ox. Address all problems in hand as quickly as possible, any delays could be detrimental. The sooner the work is done the better the result will be. The Ox will be faced with too many opinions towards the end of the month, which could be confusing. Seek professional advice in order to prevent a big loss in the very near future.

Finances are in decline. Don't gamble, keep the cash in hand, as there could be unexpected expenses at the end of the month.

The Ox is quite fit this month. Care should be taken whilst participating in outdoor activity. Beware both fire and water.

Sheep Month (13th July – 10th August)

Cheats never prosper

Various obstacles will frustrate the Ox, particularly as there seems to be no way around them. Play the game, calmly, according to the rules. Don't resort to cheap tricks or cheating – this will only result in losing the game. This is not a time to oppose superiors; offer support instead, or suffer the consequences.

Brush up on communication skills, especially towards partners or clients. Show interest in and understanding of the situation; doing this will help ensure smooth relationships.

Insecurity and lack of confidence can play havoc with the Ox this month. It'll make you too sensitive to other people's opinions and actions. This is a good time for relaxation. Take a holiday. A cruise is highly recommended.

Monkey Month (11th August – 9th September)

The course of true love never runs smooth

The work environment and career development of the Ox will improve a little this month. You will receive good news towards the end of the month. This is a good time to commence work on a short-term project. It is not a suitable time to develop international business.

Finances have improved a little. There could be a small win through gambling or on the lottery, but don't expect too much.

You will face many problems in your love life. You may even consider if it is worthwhile to be in love at all, but you ought to realize that 'the course of true love never runs smooth'. Persist with this, it is true love and it is worth it.

Rooster Month (10th September – 8th October)

Punctuality is the soul of business

There will be several opportunities to make an important career breakthrough this month, added to which is the very strong support of an extremely influential person. However, the Ox will be required to deliver time and time again, consistently making the right moves, never missing a beat, and being on time all the time. The first half of the month (mid- to end September) is smoother than the second (early to mid-October).

The Ox is not feeling that fit this month. It is a good time to watch your diet and ensure hygiene standards are maintained, particularly as there is a threat of food poisoning in the middle of the month. Also take care on the roads, especially at night.

On the personal level the Ox is looking quite emotional this month. Let bygones be bygones, be more practical and rational. Don't be judgemental and don't make unnecessary comparisons.

Dog Month (9th October – 7th November)

Curiosity killed the cat

The work environment could be quite uncomfortable this month, and the Ox is likely to be in a difficult position. It would be wise not to meddle in other people's lives, in fact the Ox is strongly advised to quite frankly mind your own business, if not, you should be prepared for the consequences. In addition your lips should be sealed on all your work projects – better keep it a business secret. This is not a good time for starting new projects, you are bound to fail.

The Ox's finances are in a mess this month. It is not advisable to invest this month. Select expensive purchases carefully, there is a likelihood of being swindled.

Healthwise things are not too bad for the Ox this month, but you should not put yourself in dangerous situations just to satisfy your curiosity.

Pig Month (8th November – 7th December)

Comparisons are odious

Although the Ox will find that many of the obstacles have been removed from daily life, remain alert to sudden changes which are likely to take place in the middle of the month. There is this ongoing tendency to constantly compare; it is better to change this attitude quickly, otherwise it will form the basis of jealous and suspicious thoughts. The primary concern for the Ox this month is to improve communication with colleagues, thus eliminating unnecessary misunderstandings.

Finances will be up and down like a roller coaster this month. Lady luck is simply not on the side of the Ox, so don't be tempted to gamble or make any investments, even though friends appear to be making money.

The Ox is entangled in several romantic relationships this

month. Try to settle down as soon as possible to avoid hurting anyone unnecessarily. Remember, stop comparing notes.

Mouse Month (8th December 1999 – 6th January 2000)

If the cap fits wear it

This is the most fortunate month for the Ox in what has not been a very good year. Outside help will bring an unexpected boost in career matters, and there will be several good offers. Look at what is available, don't be too picky – 'if the cap fits, wear it' – or several very good opportunities could be lost. The diligence of the Ox and the help of a friend will make it possible for a breakthrough this month, but keep alert – there are still more troubles ahead at the end of the year.

The health of the Ox is quite good this month. Several domestic issues need attention this month, particularly the personal care of members of the family. Pay attention to home safety and beware of fire at home.

The Ox will feel the need to complain about your partner. This will lead you on a road to nowhere, and could cause you to be isolated. It is advisable to stop this complaining quickly and remember, the cup is either half full or half empty.

Ox Month (7th January – 4th February 2000)

The road to hell is paved with good intentions

The Ox will be filled with good intentions to help others this month, but it may be wise to reconsider the entire project before proceeding. These good intentions could be wasted and you could become so absorbed by them that you could be lead blindly down a dead end street. The message is clear: don't attempt to do anything that could prove too big to handle. In addition the Ox needs to focus on immediate issues since the business traps are already set for the end of the year.

Finances will reach their lowest ebb this month. Conserve, don't spend. The extravagant habits of the Ox could be disastrous.

In matters of the heart the Ox is very emotional this month. Keep alert and try not to be blinded by sweet talk. This liaison could be as dangerous as a blind person walking along the edge of a very steep cliff.

Chapter Three

The

Tiger

Years of the Tiger

Please keep in mind when consulting the list below that the Chinese New Year begins in early February – for example, in 1962 'the year of the Tiger' covers the period 4th February 1962 to 3rd February 1963. See chart, page xv.

1914	1962
1926	1974
1938	1986
1950	1998

Distribution of the Stars within the Sign for 1999

Lucky Stars	Unlucky Stars
None	Illness Spell
	The God of Death

Please refer to pages 194–213 for traditional Chinese origins of and meanings for these Stars.

General Overview of the Year

The year is off to a good if challenging start for the Tiger. In terms of career, finances and romance, diplomacy is the key.

The Rabbit month will be particularly auspicious – though Tigers need to heed advice regarding their health. There are further complications and resistance during the Dragon and Snake months, though these stresses will ease considerably during the summer (Horse and Sheep) months.

The month of the Monkey sees the rumblings of autumn storms. Internal disputes and office politics will create many challenges for the Tiger. The Rooster month will see Tigers hit their lowest point of the year – tensions will come to a head, which could have repercussions on the Tiger's health.

The months of the Dog, Pig and Mouse will be less fraught, and the Tiger's load will be lightened. Tigers will be called upon to inspire and advance the causes of others, which will be to everyone's benefit.

The Tiger will see a happy ending to this rather troublesome year, at last, with increased strength and the wherewithal to forge ahead with plans, hopes and desires.

Monthly In-depth Forecasts
Tiger Month (16th February – 17th March)

Experience keeps a dear school

The important message this month is to learn from others, this will help prevent the Tiger from making unnecessary mistakes. The way the Tiger handles business is vital, you will need to pay attention to details to eliminate the margin of error, which could have a costly effect. In order to maintain a steady progress in business it is necessary to reach an agreement with superiors, so agree future plans – including responsibilities. Overall keep a low profile this month, and don't expect too much. This way the Tiger will alleviate the disappointment which comes from rejection.

The finances of the Tiger will get better and better this month. This is not a license to spend madly; watch the expenses or the bank balance could end up in the red by month's end.

On the social scene Tigers will be very popular, and you will have a romantic month. But, your partner is keeping a very close eye on you so you ought to be alert, and faithful. To fail to heed this advice, now, could mean months of trouble ahead.

Rabbit Month (18th March – 15th April)

Thrift is a great source of revenue

This promises to be the most auspicious month for the Tiger. Your career will run smoothly and you can expect outside help. In fact there is an excellent chance of promotion, particularly if you have fostered and maintained a good working relationship with superiors. But it is not only superiors who are important; pay attention to subordinates, too, or risk the possibility of being excluded. If the Tiger has any desire to start a new project or change career direction this is an excellent month to do so. Don't forget to keep business activities secret.

Finances will be exceptional this month. Investments will yield positive returns. Don't forget to put some aside for a rainy day – remember – 'thrift is a great source of revenue'.

In the area of health and safety, watch your diet or you could develop stomach problems. There is also a warning regarding home safety – so check alarm systems and particularly be on the alert for fire.

Dragon Month (16th April – 14th May)

Don't get mad – get even

This is a challenging month for the Tiger, filled with resistance and objections. There is also likely to be some unfair treatment. It is in the best interests of the Tiger to remain tranquil and unruffled in this critical period. Creating a harmonious environment could prevent ruination. Ensure peaceful relationships are maintained. Routine tasks should be handled with care. Verify all important documents and contracts. Remember, don't get mad, look for a fair deal.

Finances too will be in regression. So, don't risk any hard earned cash on gambling or investments, watch your budget instead. Don't be blinded by 'get rich quick' schemes which could end up disastrously.

On the personal front, if your partner seems to treat you unfairly this month, let it be – don't get mad. If handled carefully the Tiger's partner will soon return to his or her normal loving self.

Snake Month (15th May – 13th June)

Haste is the road to hell

Day-to-day tasks could present some complications for the Tiger this month. Approach these problems logically, slowly and carefully. Patience is called for, as any hastily made decisions could lead nowhere. Opportunities will present themselves – scrutinize each one of them as there could be some deception involved.

Examine all personal old bad habits this month and, if possible, give them up. I am referring to overindulging, drinking and smoking. These things can seriously damage the health of the Tiger, and this month the signs are beginning to show. Go to the doctor for an annual check-up.

The Tiger is hot-headed and petulant this month. Every effort must be made to treat friends and family in a convivial, good-natured manner. If you feel you cannot be friendly, then I suggest you take a break until you can behave in a more kind-hearted way.

Horse Month (14th June – 12th July)

It's easy to be wise after the event

At last, the problems of the last few months will begin to dissolve. For the whole of this month, the road ahead is wide and smooth. Many people will approach the Tiger with good advice this month, but actually the advice is useless because 'it is easy to be wise after the event.' Potential for career development will be good; the trick is to spot the potential and make the most of the opportunity. It could serve the Tiger in good stead later. Good news will arrive from overseas.

The Tiger's finances are much improved this month. A small bonus is likely to be received this month.

Travel plans look good for this month. Any holiday will be very pleasant, but watch what you eat!

Sheep Month (13th July – 10th August)

Better to have more friends than enemies

The Tiger's career development continues to do well this month. However, towards the middle of the month the Tiger will face some personal relationship issues. This is due to the appearance, in Chinese Traditional Astrology, of 'Heavenly Incantation'. Maintaining harmonious relationships is an extremely important factor for success; the way to achieve harmony is through friendliness and forgiveness. Bear in mind 'it is better to have more friends than enemies.'

The immune system of the Tiger will be weak this month. Watch personal hygiene and try to keep away from people with infections.

Don't expect too much in your love life either, let bygones be bygones. If your partner has left you, it could be better to start afresh, rather than trying to salvage the situation.

Monkey Month (11th August – 9th September)

It's an ill bird that fouls its own nest

There are some troubles in the nest: it may be time to do a performance appraisal for partners and subordinates, as there could be some bad eggs about. These people could well destroy the equilibrium the Tiger has been working so hard to maintain. Action should be taken to get rid of the bad eggs; this action could help to settle the internal disputes which seem to be occurring. If not, outside competition is getting tougher and the Tiger might well make the decision: 'if you can't beat 'em, join 'em'.

Finances will drop sharply this month. Be more conservative regarding financial matters. Better to keep cash in hand for unexpected expenses.

Health is poor. If the Tiger is going hunting or swimming all safety measures need to put in place, in fact any outdoor activities need to be planned and executed carefully.

Rooster Month (10th September – 8th October)

Constant dripping wears away a stone

This will not be a fortunate month for the Tiger. The continuous and ongoing pressures – business, financial and personal – are beginning to take their toll. Tigers should do whatever they need to do to equip themselves psychologically in order to keep a positive attitude. Try not to slide into negativity as the constant dripping of water on stone can gradually cause the stone to crumble.

Healthwise it appears that you have reached the end of your tether and could be heading for a nervous breakdown. Let common sense prevail, don't take on any additional stress by continuing to burn the candle at both ends. If possible take a holiday and relax.

Friendships are fraught with tension. Try to introduce some happiness and laughter; this is more possible in a relaxed environment. This will go a long way towards keeping important relationships from crumbling.

Dog Month (9th October – 7th November)

Early to bed early to rise makes a man healthy, wealthy and wise

Tigers are much better off this month. A chance for some real career achievement is probable, and personal problems are fast disappearing. Approach business meetings and conventions with much more enthusiasm; this will help to broaden your knowledge and build connections. Business dealings in foreign countries will develop well. The third quarter of the year is looking good.

Finances are on the way up. In fact your economic crisis will be over if you can cut down on unnecessary expenses. However, don't be too hesitant to take a calculated risk, or an excellent opportunity to make some extra money could be lost.

Health is taking a turn for the better. The Tiger will probably want to get lots of rest. This is nature's way of healing, so indulge in beautiful sleep.

Pig Month (8th November – 7th December)

Do unto others as you would have them do unto you

This is the time for spreading a little goodwill. Be generous, considerate and kind to other people. You will find that the way you treat clients and colleagues will be reflected in the way your clients and colleagues treat you. Precision time-keeping is needed too, specifically when it comes to meetings. This impeccable behaviour will impress influential people and will lead the Tiger down the road to success.

Health is on the decline again. It is important to watch your diet and be careful of what and when you eat, because food poisoning is a threat. Elderly members of the family may need some special attention, don't hesitate to take them to the doctor or clinic when they need to go.

Be more considerate of loved ones, this will make the Tiger very popular and meet with strong approval. A very active social period is indicated.

Mouse Month (8th December 1999 – 6th January 2000)

Hope deferred makes the heart sick

Work closely with colleagues this month, they will be drawing strength from the Tiger. So, amongst the difficulties which present themselves in day-to-day activities, you will be required to offer much inspiration and encouragement. Keep in mind that 'hope deferred makes the heart sick'. Honour any promises which you may have made, and give praise when praise is due. This is not a good month for making major changes in business.

The Tiger's finances are very poor this month. Applications for loans or mortgages may be turned down. Try to pay bills promptly to avoid any trouble later.

On the romantic front, you must keep promises to loved ones if you wish to have a trouble-free and peaceful relationship. Be on the alert for a love triangle which may be developing.

Ox Month (7th January – 4th February 2000)

Things past cannot be recalled

The predictions for the Tiger are not very good this year, but 1999 does have a happy ending. Plan ahead for the future, and make sure to look forward all the time, not backwards. Concentrate on strengthening and forging relationships with associates and clients. This is an excellent month to start a new business venture or project.

By and large the health of the Tiger persists in being below par. Little aches and pains, like headaches, toothache and stomach ache continue to pester you. Really it makes sense to get plenty of rest.

Don't be depressed if there is a breakdown in a relationship with a loved one. It is probably for the best. Relax and let bygones be bygones.

Chapter Four

兎

The
Rabbit

Years of the Rabbit

Please keep in mind when consulting the list below that the Chinese New Year begins in early February – for example, in 1963 'the year of the Rabbit' covers the period 4th February 1963 to 3rd February 1964. And if born in 1915, 1927 or 1939, the year begins on 5th February.

1915	1963
1927	1975
1939	1987
1951	1999

Distribution of the Stars within the Sign for 1999

Lucky Star	Unlucky Stars
The Star of Commander	Heavenly Weeping
	Watch-dog of the Year
	Sword's Edge
	Lying Corpse

Please refer to pages 194–213 for traditional Chinese origins of and meanings for these Stars.

General Overview of the Year

The first three months of the year are excellent for the Rabbit. The Tiger month is a good time to mount new ventures and begin to branch out into new areas of interest – such pursuits will go well in this first month. In the second month (the month of the Rabbit) things get slightly rocky but the Rabbit's persistence and charm win through. The month of the Dragon sees Rabbits in peak condition, able to fight off all competition and at their most persuasive.

The months of the Snake and Horse will bring their share of traumas: frustrations at work and home will contribute to the Rabbit's general sense of going nowhere slowly. Rabbits must gird themselves during these months for a struggle.

The summer months (months of the Sheep and Monkey) will be fun-filled and active ones. There will be plenty of opportunities for advancement, but the Rabbit will be more interested in kicking back and enjoying life. The autumn (months of the Rooster, Dog and Pig) is the time for more careful consideration and caution, as progress slows and there could be unseen enemies afoot. Rabbits must mind their temper.

The last two months (of the Mouse and Ox) see an upturn for the Rabbit. After long struggles Rabbits reap the financial, professional and emotional rewards, and end the year on a high note.

Monthly In-depth Forecasts
Tiger Month (16th February – 17th March)

It takes two to make a bargain

The year starts well for the Rabbit. 1999 is an excellent time to start something new, a new job, change of career or business venture. There will not be many obstacles to overcome and generally all business matters will run smoothly and without interference. The Rabbit is in the perfect position for negotiating a deal. You must make use of this bargaining power, taking into account any advantages over your competition. The Rabbit should be seeking long-term benefits.

Financially the Rabbit will be pretty well off this month. You will be lucky in investments and in gambling, but don't be too greedy. There will be an even bigger profit if you decide to work harmoniously with your business partners.

Rabbits will be actively involved in social activity. Others will find you very attractive; as a result this could be a very romantic month for you.

Rabbit Month (18th March – 15th April)

Divide and rule

Diversification is the name of the game for the Rabbit this month. The Rabbit should not only concentrate on one project this month but develop ideas regarding related business opportunities. This will stand you in good stead later.

Finances are not as rosy as they were last month. Your income will be stable, but you should take care not to put all your eggs in one basket.

There will be some conflicts on the home front this month. Sort these conflicting opinions out by individually addressing each person's grievances. A collective solution won't work. This is a good time to establish who qualifies as a true friend, or a true partner. Be alert to wolves in sheep's clothing.

Dragon Month (16th April – 14th May)

Actions speak louder than words

It will be in the Rabbit's best interest to persuade superiors and clients to accept business proposals which will secure the best possible results in the months ahead. Never forgetting that 'actions speak louder than words', if the Rabbit fails to deliver then the support gained now will be lost sooner or later. Don't mix business with pleasure, things could get very messy. Overall this will be a productive and rewarding month for the Rabbit.

The Rabbit is in peak condition this month. Any dangers will come from outside – be aware of personal safety, don't walk alone on quiet streets at night. There is a threat of robbery or violence.

Empty promises will not be taken lightly by loved ones and friends. Take steps to fulfil any promises made to a partner or spouse.

Snake Month (15th May – 13th June)

There's no great loss without some gain

The first three months of the year have been excellent for the Rabbit, but don't get too ambitious or hasty – there will be some traumas ahead this month. An important decision needs to be made; contemplate all the elements regarding this situation and seek the help of professionals if necessary. Furthermore a series of difficulties, also involving business, will present itself this month. Solve these difficulties with the help of associates, don't try to fix them single-handedly, they will prove too much for you.

Finances look miserable this month. Formulate a conservative budget, don't gamble or invest, and don't participate in any 'get rich quick' schemes.

The frustrations of work may be taking their toll on personal relationships. Set work matters aside on the home front and show some love and affection.

Horse Month (14th June – 12th July)

If you want peace you must prepare for war

Here's a challenge. You must equip yourself by preparing for a hard struggle with your opponents, rivals or competitors. The Rabbit will face strong adversity in the first 20 days of this month. My advice is to stand firm, hold your ground, and don't give up too much – you will be labelled a coward, by the opposition, if you do. This firm stance will scare off competition, especially when they witness first-hand your clear will to succeed. Therefore if Rabbits are looking for peace they should first prepare for war.

The financial situation is in decline for the Rabbit. And there will be unexpected bills to pay at month's end.

Healthwise there are no major problems, but take care when outdoors – especially so if hunting, swimming and diving are involved.

Sheep Month (13th July – 10th August)

Business before pleasure

Excellent opportunities for change, or for new business, are presenting themselves. But the Rabbit is in the mood for pleasure and will tend to spend more time playing than working. In fact that is your dilemma: how to co-ordinate business with pleasure – the best rule is 'business before pleasure.' Indulge in pleasurable activities outside of working hours, or take a holiday, but only do this once major business responsibilities have been attended to. The Rabbit must make sure a well-briefed, hand-picked candidate is appointed to stand in your absence since your rivals would love to take advantage of your absence.

Finances are looking better and there is the likelihood of a good return on short-term investments.

Rabbits are in high spirits. You will be actively engaged in social gatherings with friends and family. That's fine, but don't allow pleasure to interfere with business.

Monkey Month (11th August – 9th September)

A penny saved is a penny earned

Broader business plans will run very smoothly this month. Concentrate on day-to-day issues. Most importantly, the Rabbit must look after the company's budget, paying specific attention to wasteful expenditure as this could lead to a deficit balance at year end. This is the most suitable month to concentrate on company expenses – remember, 'a penny saved is a penny earned'. There is no necessity to cut down on valid expenses or on the overall budget as this could later damage the company.

Saving money is the most important thing for the Rabbit to do this month. There is no point in pursuing additional income when you cannot control your current spending.

Rabbits should try solving the conflicts which still exist between family and friends. Never let an argument escalate into violence. Advisedly, Rabbits must avoid disputes of any kind this month.

Rooster Month (10th September – 8th October)

There are tricks in every trade

Rabbits could easily be tricked this month. The Rabbit must walk slowly and carefully, avoid making a hasty decision and thereby putting career or business at risk. It seems that some individuals are out to trick the Rabbit into submission. Hopefully you have learned the tricks of your trade very well, and are in a position to deal with these threats. If at all doubtful seek professional help. Be conservative in business this month.

Finances are poor at this time. Try not to make any investments; they could end in tears.

In affairs of the heart don't be fooled by a pretty face. Rabbits must exercise common sense when choosing a partner. Sincerity is the quality which the Rabbit should be seeking.

Dog Month (9th October – 7th November)

Half a loaf is better than none

Progress in business slows down. Don't worry about this, a little is better than nothing at all. Don't push too hard or be too ambitious, it will backfire. Make sure that your behaviour is impeccable as there is a tendency for others to talk behind your back. Avoid heated discussions or arguments. Remember that as long as you are innocent you have nothing to worry about.

Be content with less income and less luxury this month – 'half a loaf is better than none'.

Health is fine, but remember safety first. Be on the look-out for danger from fire and water.

Pig Month (8th November – 7th December)

Never let the sun go down on your anger

Rabbits could be easily irritated by continuous conflicts with superiors and clients. Keep your temper under control, this is a sensitive time to show a burst of anger and the consequences could be serious. The best thing to do is to convert your anger into self-motivation, thereby strengthening your resolve. This will enable a good result at the end of the year.

Don't waste energy on anger this month, it can be very draining. Instead you should try to calm yourself. Be careful if driving or walking in the white heat caused by rage.

Rabbits must stay calm and placid towards their family, certainly do not take anger out on them. The situation will worsen if you do. It is worthwhile repeating 'don't let the sun go down on your anger'.

Mouse Month (8th December 1999 – 6th January 2000)

No pain, no gain

The last two months once again take an up-turn for the Rabbit. Hard work will pay dividends this month, idleness will result in nothing. Any conflicts with clients must be resolved; creating a harmonious work environment will mean an important breakthrough at year end.

Finances are upwardly mobile once again. Investing in various areas, at this time, will yield good profits. Be careful to choose the right project to begin with.

Your love life is given a refreshing lift this month. Be courageous about expressing the true feelings of love which the Rabbit has been keeping inside. Be prepared for a wonderful surprise.

Ox Month (7th January – 4th February 2000)

Better late than never

It has been a long struggle for the Rabbit this year. Dreams do come true and the Rabbit's dreams all come true at the end of the year, 'better late than never'. Make sure all important meetings are attended – failure to attend will hurt your career or business activities. This is a fabulous time for you to reconsider your future developments, as you will have a crystal-clear perception of what, and where, you want to be.

It seems that the Rabbit's immunity is weak this month, so extra care will need to be taken with your health, particularly when fighting illnesses. So wrap up warm and watch what you eat.

Go on, be demonstrative. The Rabbit should not be afraid of showing affection, it will be rewarded doubly. It may be a little late, but 'better late than never'.

Chapter Five

The

Dragon

Years of the Dragon

Please keep in mind when consulting the list below that the Chinese New Year begins in early February – for example, in 1964 'the year of the Dragon' covers the period 5th February 1964 to 3rd February 1965. See chart page xv.

1904	1952
1916	1964
1928	1976
1940	1988

Distribution of the Stars within the Sign for 1999

Lucky Stars **Unlucky Star**

The Sun Black Cloud

Commander's Saddle

Please refer to pages 194–213 for traditional Chinese origins of and meanings for these Stars.

General Overview of the Year

The Dragon's challenge at the start of the year (Tiger month) is to embrace change and see its upside – then the Dragon will be able to reap the benefits. The second month (month of the Rabbit) will see many difficulties fall by the wayside: this is the time for forward planning. In the month of the Dragon, it will be necessary to try to open up to different points of view – the key to success in what will be a rather trying time.

The month of the Snake will be a difficult one for the Dragon: keep calm and proceed with due deliberation. The month of the Horse will continue stormy; Dragons will need all their patience and perseverance, but they will succeed if they can keep their temper in check. Things improve in the month of the Sheep, though there will still be conflicts. Nevertheless, finances and social aspirations are looking up. The month of the Monkey is a time for diplomacy in all things.

The month of the Rooster will be most fortunate for the Dragon. Many opportunities will be revealed – the Dragon's task will be to choose among them wisely. The month of the Dog will be a difficult one: Dragons must arm themselves for combat.

The last three months of the year will pose very few problems, coming as a blessed relief after what has been an up-and-down year. These months see an upturn financially, personally and professionally. Business is booming, love is blooming, and finances are in good shape. Just be careful about burning the candle at both ends – Dragons should take breaks from the routine whenever possible; it will do everyone good.

Monthly In-depth Forecasts
Tiger Month (16th February – 17th March)

You cannot put new wine in old bottles

Dragons should not be so reluctant to change this month. Change is inevitable, it would be very wise for the Dragon to embrace new ideas and new technology in order to not only survive but to maintain the leading edge.

Communication and meetings with partners is recommended. This is not the time for new projects or for persuading superiors to take on new projects – trying to put old wine into new bottles is entirely inappropriate and will do much harm.

You are not at your healthiest, wrap up warm to avoid a chill. Keep away from too much alcohol and drugs, and don't risk walking into a dead-end street.

You are inclined to be quite cool towards your partner this month, and this could cause conflict. It is advisable to seek a third person in whom you can confide – this could save the relationship.

Rabbit Month (18th March – 15th April)

Good seed makes a good crop

Difficulties experienced last month will melt away like snow on a sunny day. This month business will run very smoothly as all obstacles have been removed. The Dragon has the opportunity, through hard work, to be very successful this year. The primary task which the Dragon should tackle this month is forward planning, both in business and financial matters. You should choose good projects to start this month, just as the farmer would choose good seeds for cultivation in early spring, thus ensuring a good harvest at year end.

This is a good month for finances. It is a good time to purchase property. Applications for loans or mortgages will be approved without any problems. There will be a satisfactory return on investments. Chances of winning a lottery are good towards the end of the month.

Demonstrate affection towards your spouse or partner; in early spring this will yield a wonderful surprise. However, if the Dragon has several relationships happening at the same time, it could be likened to planting many weeds in the garden, and there will be a lot of tidying up to do later.

Dragon Month (16th April – 14th May)

A fool may give a wise man counsel

Communication includes criticism; Dragons will be wise to open up to different perspectives. The ideas of others could inspire your own creativity. Keep in mind that even a fool can give advice to a wise man. Do some client research, talk to them, gather their opinions, this will help you to understand their demands. Beware cleverly disguised hypocrites.

Finances will be a little less robust this month, so refrain from gambling or investing. Some serious thinking will need to be done before purchasing luxury products or some money could be lost.

The health of the Dragon is slightly better than it has been. Road safety looks threatening, so be careful driving or walking.

Snake Month (15th May – 13th June)

Know thyself

The two months of the year which are most unfortunate for the Dragon are May and September. Try to resolve problems wisely and quickly, don't allow the situation to continue.

It could be easy to get lost amongst all the invitations and temptations which the Dragon will face this month. Keep calm. Reconsider the situation carefully. If you are familiar with your own weaknesses, and shortcomings, this knowledge will help in strengthening your willpower, rendering you unbeatable. Competition is fierce for the next three months and you will need to protect yourself against this.

The Dragon's health is good this month. Personal safety is of primary importance, especially around water. When swimming or fishing, don't go alone; try to have an experienced swimmer around.

There will be an opportunity to meet an attractive member of the opposite sex, but the water will need to be tested before going any further, as disappointment may follow. Be honest and sincere to both old and new partners; it is always better and will be appreciated in the future.

Horse Month (14th June – 12th July)

Be patient and endure

The problems facing the Dragon are difficult to handle; patience and endurance will be necessary to sustain equilibrium. Should you give in too easily you will lose the respect of your peers and leave the door open for the competition. Try not to provoke superiors; if they prove to be picky this month be patient and try to convince them of your point of view slowly.

Finances could be in a critical position if you do not watch your expenses. Your budget will need to be managed prudently, and additional income should be sorted out. Don't test your luck by gambling.

The Dragon will be quick-tempered this month and this could cause unnecessary conflict with friends and partners. Try to be more patient and even-tempered in order to settle personal issues.

Sheep Month (13th July – 10th August)

It is better to give than to receive

Whilst there are still some problems which need solving, the work environment will improve this month. The Dragon may be invited to form a joint venture of some kind – refrain, this is not the right time, give it a little more consideration. There will be opportunities for frequent travel, though the Dragon ought to be careful of business traps whilst in foreign countries. Rely on business partners to help, don't take on the entire burden yourself.

The Dragon's finances are looking better this month. Assist those who are constantly asking for a helping hand – they will repay you with great generosity. Remember, it is always better to give than to receive.

The Dragon will be quite healthy this month. Be careful of seafood as there could be a possibility of food poisoning. Watch youngsters, particularly in the water; make sure they are accompanied by an adult.

Monkey Month (11th August – 9th September)

Charity begins at home

There will not be any sudden upheavals in business development this month. In order to improve the chances of a marked success this year it would be wise to concentrate on human relations, and this is a good time to do so. Make sure you are on the same wavelength as partners and that the situation is harmonious. This stable relationship will secure the future. This is a good time to start preparing for business development in winter.

The financial situation of the Dragon is still good this month. You could win a lottery. Be generous to the poor or family members who may ask for help. Also demonstrate care and physical affection particularly to the family – remember, charity begins at home.

Rooster Month (10th September – 8th October)

Fair and softly goes far in a day

This will be a most fortunate month for the Dragon. Several opportunities will open up. Choose carefully the one which best meets your long-term objectives. Making the wrong choice will prove costly. Be convivial to colleagues and subordinates – your support will go a long way to ensuring career advancement. Keep in mind that 'fair and softly' will take you much further in the long run.

Dragons are healthy and in peak condition this month. A balanced diet and lower alcohol intake will help you to maintain this condition, and will strengthen your immune system, thereby helping to fight infections.

Your love life and social life are looking good, provided you continue to be friendly to all those with whom you associate.

Dog Month (9th October – 7th November)

A burnt child dreads fire

This is a difficult month for the Dragon. You will need to arm yourself for the battle with your superiors, and rivals. If you do not know how to protect yourself you will be badly beaten. This will cause you to lose your confidence just like 'a burnt child dreads fire'. You will need to find a way to rebuild your confidence if you should suffer defeat. Think positively and look forward, the next three months are extremely fortunate.

There will be a sudden drop in finances, and, like a thunderstorm, this will come without any warning. Dragons should be very conservative with money. Save your money as one might save food for the coming winter.

Where love is concerned this is not a month to 'fool around'. This will be playing with fire, and the Dragon will get badly burnt.

Pig Month (8th November – 7th December)

Fortune favours the brave

Last month's thunderstorm will disappear totally, and with it the problems which the Dragon has had to overcome – like a shadow vanishes when the sunshine appears. The last quarter of the year presents few obstacles, and is an excellent time for the Dragon to embark on new projects, or to change careers. You will need to muster all your courage to take this chance, but risk it you must or possibly end up with nothing. A calculated risk will do you no harm at all. Remember that fortune favours the brave.

Finances have improved, so new money can be invested in new projects. Be alert to people who would be happy to deceive.

This is the right time to express your true feelings to a loved one. You will be astonished by the response to this behaviour. So, pluck up the courage and say what you feel.

Mouse Month (8th December 1999 – 6th January 2000)

The sea never refuses water

Business is booming for the Dragon this month. A word of caution: don't become complacent or blinded by success. Exercise humility and modesty or risk the chance of isolation, which will harm your future prosperity. Dragons must be open to change and listen to the opinions of others – even the sea never refuses extra water. A narrow-minded person will never become a great person and never really achieve much.

The fortune of the Dragon is excellent this month. There will be a good return on investments, but spend conservatively at month's end.

Jealousy and suspicion will easily be aroused in the Dragon this month. This destructive behaviour could severely damage or completely ruin relationships. Do whatever is necessary to avoid these feelings, which eat away like a cancer.

Ox Month (7th January – 4th February 2000)

Easy does it

Take a break from the normal routine and enjoy a month with family and friends if this is at all possible. Try not to work too hard – better not to burn the candle at both ends. An exhausted person cannot be effective. Better to let someone else take over the responsibilities for the time being, or you will end up picking on small people and small problems, something which you can well do without. Take a break and avoid the problems.

Whilst on this happy holiday period, try not to drink too much alcohol. Take all the personal safety precautions such as driving carefully and locking all windows and doors of the car and the house.

Include loved ones in these travels abroad. It will be a wonderful holiday. Be mindful of pickpockets, and make sure passports are kept in a safe place.

Chapter Six

The

Snake

Years of the Snake

Please keep in mind when consulting the list below that the Chinese New Year begins in early February – for example, in 1965 'the year of the Snake' covers the period 4th February 1965 to 3rd February 1966.

1905	1953
1917	1965
1929	1977
1941	1989

Distribution of the Stars within the Sign for 1999

Lucky Star	Unlucky Stars
Travelling Horse	God of Loneliness
	Funeral's Door
	Threat of Disasters

Please refer to pages 194–213 for traditional Chinese origins of and meanings for these Stars.

General Overview of the Year

The first month of the year (Tiger month) finds the snake scrambling to rebuild a shaky self-esteem. In the pursuit of ambitions and goals, the Snake will have to learn to find the strength of spirit to face up to challenges from all quarters. In the Rabbit month, Snakes will have to have their wits about them if they are to defeat rival claims and conflicts of interest.

The Dragon month sees an upturn in the Snake's fortune, particularly regarding finances and career. Flexibility is important, as is stamina, if the Snake is to make the most of this lucky streak. Diligence and flair during the month of the Snake will reap many rewards.

The months of the Horse and Sheep will be a testing time for Snakes. They must try to root out weaknesses and imperfections, and put their houses in order. Caution and tenacity should be the bywords. Accept help when it is offered – and if it is not offered, ask for it!

The month of the Monkey will be one of the best periods in the Snake's year. Many opportunities will present themselves – the trick is to choose wisely. This is the time for putting career or professional plans and projects into place. The month of the Rooster will see increased competition – if Snakes have prepared well, they should be able to see this off. The month of the Dog will be the most fortunate of the year. Business is running smoothly and finances are looking good.

The last three months of the year (Pig, Mouse and Ox months) will pose certain difficulties for the Snake. Careful preparation will avert many problems before they get out of hand. In unity lies strength: personal and professional partnerships will prosper everyone involved. Snakes must stand their ground if they are to see the old year out with increased vigour and optimism for the future.

Monthly In-depth Forecasts
Tiger Month (16th February – 17th March)

Faint heart never won fair lady

The Snake seems to have lost confidence; this year you need to spend some time rebuilding it. You have a tendency to step back and avoid facing difficulties – this will be a major stumbling block for you if you wish to achieve your goals. Gather all your courage to take a chance in your career or an excellent chance could slip through your fingers. There will be a much better chance for achievement if you dare to accept the challenge. This is not the time for a low profile, be pro-active and participate in business matters.

Finances will not be so favourable this month. This is not a good time for risking money in any kind of investment, and there is no luck to be had in gambling, so the Snake should save money as one would save water for coming drought.

Don't be too shy and passive, in love, this month. A 'faint heart' won't win the attention of a fair lady.

Rabbit Month (18th March – 15th April)

Fools build houses and wise men live in them

You will have to use your intelligence to outwit rivals, or be beaten into submission. You will find it exceedingly difficult to restore your credibility if you allow yourself to be beaten by greedy opportunists. In other words, the Snake will need to prevent 'wise men' from occupying the house built with blood, sweat and tears. Clearly this is not a good month for the Snake to start a new project or a new business – wait until the Autumn.

The finances of the Snake will be very poor this month. Keep away from potential financial traps; beware of deception.

As usual the health of the Snake will be very good. However, keep an eye on youngsters, take good care of them and ensure they receive proper treatment if they should display any signs of illness.

Dragon Month (16th April – 14th May)

Fortune favours the brave

Financial luck and business affairs both look good for the Snake this month. Once again, muster up the courage to take the chance – it will pay dividends. If the Snake feels that taking on extra responsibility will be too much to handle, then invite a partner on board – share the load. Too much hesitation will only give the impression of cowardice. Remember 'fortune favours the brave'.

Finances are much improved this month, but whether the Snake will make a fortune depends on the Snake's decision to take a calculated investment risk or not.

Be more flexible towards your partner, if you want to maintain a peaceful private life. The end of the month is a suitable time to take a holiday with your loved one.

Snake Month (15th May – 13th June)

Where bees are, there is honey

The Snake will have to work hard to earn respect. The harder you work, the more you will receive. You have to use your intelligence to detect hidden opportunities and, having found them, make the most of them. Just as the bees will seek out the prettiest flowers, and then work diligently to make honey out of them, so should the Snake. The honey should be stored for winter, as this could be a cold and bad period for the Snake. There are some good business opportunities developing abroad – not surprisingly, then, this is a good time to develop overseas interests.

The Snake is in pretty good health. You need to take care at times of dramatic weather changes, and be aware of the dangers of wild animals and strong rivers.

There is a good chance that the Snake will meet an influential person this month. It will be in the Snake's interests to befriend this person and win his or her support. This is not a good month for romance.

Horse Month (14th June – 12th July)

A stitch in time saves nine

This is a testing month for your business ventures. Prepare for a better time next month – the more prepared you are, the more secure the future will be. Work on building confidence; a positive approach is needed to handle difficulties in the months ahead. Don't forget, 'a stitch in time saves nine'.

Snakes should look out for weaknesses in their financial system. You will need to find a way to prevent money from leaking away, and you should do this sooner rather than later.

Conflicts between you and your lover will become more and more obvious. Take action to prevent the situation from deteriorating. A mutual understanding is best.

Sheep Month (13th July – 10th August)

A burnt child dreads fire

This is one of the most unfortunate months for the Snake. Exercise caution, and handle day-to-day activities with precision and care. Don't play with fire, as it can burn away your confidence. If you have faced a defeat this month, you will have to triumph over this stumbling block in order to even stronger challenges next month. Don't be afraid to ask for help.

The finances of the Snake will be threatened this month. Save money for a rainy day. Whilst travelling, take care of personal belongings.

Don't talk too much about friends or lovers behind their backs, as this will result in some serious pain – for you.

Monkey Month (11th August – 9th September)

Time and tide wait for no man

This is one of the best periods for the Snake this year. There are may opportunities to choose from – the trick is to choose wisely and quickly. Missed opportunities will be gone for ever: 'time and tide wait for no man.'

The time is right to start a new project or change career direction. Fight for your future and your rights, because no one else is around to fight on your behalf.

Money matters are looking pretty good. The possibility exists for a very good return on short-term investments, and there could be some luck in gambling.

Tell the 'love of your life' how important he or she is to you. This action will stimulate positive communication. Timing is important, so be alert to the correct time and place, or it could pass by as swiftly and invisibly as the wind.

Rooster Month (10th September – 8th October)

Do right and fear no man

Competition is tough this month. You will need to apply yourself in order to beat the competition. There will be much criticism aimed at the Snake – the best thing to do is concentrate on business. Very simply, 'do right and fear no man'. Don't allow the critics to interfere with your original plans. This is an appropriate time for Snakes to re-organize their personal and business schedule.

The Snake's health is below par this month. Try to stick to a regular healthy routine, eat well and get plenty of rest and enough sleep. Beyond that, watch out for falling objects.

Stand firmly alongside your partner or spouse this month, make sure they know how you feel about them, otherwise there is a threat of this relationship ending.

Dog Month (9th October – 7th November)

Thrift is a great revenue

This will be the most fortunate time for the Snake this year. Business will run smoothly, and orders from clients will flood in. However keep an eye on quality and service, this will ensure repeat orders. Keep production and operating costs under control, in fact all overheads should be contained, to contain the impact on future business.

Although the financial situation of the Snake looks good this month, cut back, thriftily, on unnecessary expenses.

Be careful where you walk, an accident caused by falling, or maybe by a falling object, could happen.

Pig Month (8th November – 7th December)

It never rains but it pours

Prepare for difficulties in the last three months of this year. Problems will come very suddenly, like a thunderstorm in the tropics, without warning. So, Snakes should do all the preparation work in advance, starting with accounting systems. Clear any bad debts, and check the accounts. Double check everything in order to avoid a costly mistake. Try to settle internal disputes before they become too serious.

Don't make any investments this month, and try to stop the money from flowing out. Get out of debt and keep out of danger.

Be honest with your spouse or partner, or a misunderstanding could develop. A third party is doing his best to use this misunderstanding to his advantage.

Mouse Month (8th December 1999 – 6th January 2000)

Unity is strength

Try to create a partnership or a union this month. Facing difficulties alone is doubly difficult, and could lead to further isolation. The strength of this union will lay a solid foundation during this trying period. Focus on making this union effective. Otherwise keep a low profile and avoid being the centre of attention.

Snakes should ask for financial assistance or advice from trustworthy friends or family, if need be. Don't be too depressed, the problem will clear up later.

Don't lock yourself away from society this month, get out there and communicate with people who are meaningful. This contact will boost confidence levels and lighten the load.

Ox Month (7th January – 4th February 2000)

When things are at their worst, they begin to mend

It seems that the Snake will have no way out this month, the difficulties which you face can be quite overwhelming, BUT, the situation does change from bad to good. Just as Spring will surely come after the severest winter, so too will the Snake's life begin to mend when you feel at your worst. The Snake must not give in too easily, the one who stands his ground will win, in fact the worst enemy you have is yourself.

Finances of the Snake are at their lowest this month. This is not a problem if you have not taken any risks in gambling or investing.

You and your partner will need to turn the page and start your relationship afresh. This will probably result in a happy ending.

The

Horse

Years of the Horse

Please keep in mind when consulting the list below that the Chinese New Year begins in early February – for example, in 1954 'the year of the Horse' covers the period 4th February 1954 to 3rd February 1955.

1906	1954
1918	1966
1930	1978
1942	1990

Distribution of the Stars within the Sign in 1999

Lucky Stars	Unlucky Stars
The Moon	Hooked and Strained
Heavenly Happiness	Six Harms
	Tightened Loop
	Sudden Death

Please refer to pages 194–213 for traditional Chinese origins of and meanings for these Stars.

General Overview of the Year

Those people born in the year of the Horse will have a prosperous year in 1999. The Horse will see a very good start to the year. This good fortune will continue into the second month of the year. But there will be several difficulties near the end of the second month. They will have much better luck in the second half of the year. A word of warning: do not be caught by traps.

The months of the Dragon and Snake will be the most unfortunate period of time for the Horse. Pay special attention to your work, but mind you don't burn the candle at both ends. Apart from this, try to protect yourself from the competition.

The Horse will have a very fortunate period of time in the months of the Horse, Sheep and Monkey. You will have the chance of promotion within these three months. This will be a very good time for the Horse to start a new project.

Bad luck will come suddenly in the Rooster month. The unexpected always happens during this month. Besides this, watch out for food poisoning.

Fortunately, the Horse will have a very fortunate period of time in the last four months of the year. The Dog month will be particularly joyful. But try to keep silent about important matters. You will enjoy a sweet personal life with good health in both the Dog and Pig months.

The Horse will see splendid achievements in career matters if you concentrate on your most important project come the month of the Mouse. This will also be a very good time to make new investments.

You will win the heart of your lover easily come the Mouse month.

Throughout the year, keep an eye on your finances. Take good care of your money. You could lose a lot of money if you fall into money traps.

Business will see an important breakthrough at year end. But do not let your personal life interfere with business activities.

Do not over-indulge in alcohol or sex this year.

Take special care when you go hunting or diving.

This will be a year full of joy, and will be quite romantic for the Horse. You will be very active in social gatherings. And you will be very popular with others.

Monthly In-depth Forecasts
Tiger Month (16th February – 17th March)

Love makes the world go around

The Horse will see a very good beginning to the first month of the year. You will be active in social gatherings but you should not eat or drink too much. However, business matters will develop quite smoothly this month. You can make it even better by concentrating more on day-to-day tasks. This month will be a very suitable time to plan for your future because you will have great insight this month. Don't talk about your future developments too much, keep them as business secrets, or others will steal your ideas.

Finances will be pretty sound this month. You will have luck in lottery and gambling, but you should not be too greedy. This month is a good time for investments.

The Horse will be very popular this month. This will be a very romantic month for you. You don't have to worry about the obstacles in front of you because love will make everything go smoothly.

Rabbit Month (18th March – 15th April)

Don't count your chickens before they're hatched

The Horse will face several difficulties near the end of this month. This will be a month full of changes. A lot of unexpected things could take place. In other words, nothing is certain this month. So the Horse should double-check all the details even after the contracts have been signed, or the whole deal may be cancelled unexpectedly without notice. The best way for the Horse to proceed this month is to prepare for the worst. Try to have something in reserve as a replacement should things go pear-shaped.

Finances will witness a sudden change this month. You cannot count on your ordinary income too much. You have to keep some money by for unexpected expenses.

Do not think that your lover will never leave you. You may lose him or her suddenly if you don't seem to care about him or her too much. Don't underestimate the new intruder in your love affairs.

Dragon Month (16th April – 14th May)

Health is wealth

March and April will be the most unfortunate period of time for the Horse. You should pay special attention to your work. The Horse will be busily engaged in business activities, but try your best to have enough rest. Don't burn the candle at both ends. Your efforts and contribution will be seriously damaged if you have to take sick leave. Therefore, let others share the responsibility, so that you can be somewhat released from your heavy burden. Do not make any dramatic changes to your business this month. 'Keep it as it is' will be the best tactic for the Horse this month.

Your health will be on the edge of sudden collapse. Take care of yourself. Go on holiday if at all possible. Relax. Even a short leave will be beneficial. Don't forget that health is wealth. And health cannot be exchanged for money.

Do not over-indulge in alcohol or sex this month. Overdoing these two habits will damage your health seriously.

Snake Month (15th May – 13th June)

Self-preservation is the first law of nature

The prime concern for the Horse this month is how to protect your rights. The Horse will find out that there are so many competitors surrounding you with different intentions. It's a bit like being surrounded by wild beasts in the wilderness. Understand that 'self-preservation is the first law of nature'. You should stand firm to protect your rights. And you should not be ashamed to ask for help in an emergency. Join forces with someone who's strong enough to protect you. A firm determination and a positive attitude will help the Horse to find the way out of troubles and disputes this month.

Finances will be miserable this month. Mind your investments carefully. Better not to try your luck in gambling.

The Horse should stand up firmly to protect your lover or spouse. Your cowardice will surely devalue your image in his or her eyes.

Horse Month (14th June – 12th July)

Moderation in all things

The obstacles in front of you will be removed one by one gradually this month. But there is still a long way for the Horse to go this year. The prime concern for the Horse this month is how to stay calm when handling complicated relations among associates. Your hot temper will definitely mess up the whole thing and would make the situation even worse. Therefore, what you should do is try to be modest in all things. Humility and sincerity will resolve a lot of misunderstandings. Besides that, the Horse should aim for better communication with the people around you from now on.

Although the income of the Horse will be greatly improved, you should be conservative when it comes to financial matters.

The Horse should try not to be too emotional towards your lover and friends – this will only scare them away.

Sheep Month (13th July – 10th August)

There is always room at the top

The Horse will be promoted to a higher post this month if you work hard enough. This will be a month full of chances. Try to equip yourself with the knowledge and different skills needed to climb up step by step. There will always be room for assertive people with ability. Therefore, don't waste your chances for promotion this month. However, good relations with your associates is also important for your promotion, so don't forget about them while you're on your way up.

The Horse's finances will be very good this month. You can expect a good return on your investments. But you should not attempt to bribe your superiors for your promotion, or you could be involved in legal problems sooner or later.

The health condition of the Horse will be in pretty good shape this month. But you should watch out for your home safety. You should never leave a child alone in the house, especially towards the end of this month.

Monkey Month (11th August – 9th September)

One step at a time

The business development of the Horse this year will be going up and down like a roller coaster until September. You will face uncertainty and difficulties during July and August. You should be cautious in handling your business. There will be many business traps in front of you, so tread carefully. One step at a time. A hasty leap would be career suicide. Try to handle your business personally. And don't rely on other people too much, especially in the last two weeks of the month. If you want to change a new job or to carry out a very important project, then you should wait for the coming winter.

You should not risk your money nor your career with hasty actions. You should spend more time looking after your expenses rather than looking for additional income.

The Horse should not be too aggressive in love affairs this month. You should approach your lover with patience and care. Better not scare him or her away at the very first stage.

Rooster Month (10th September – 8th October)

The unexpected always happens

The prime concern for the Horse is try to keep alert to the possibility of the unexpected. There will be a lot of uncertainty this month, so you have to keep a close watch on your day-to-day work in order to catch any unusual developments in the early stages. The damage may be cut down to a very minor scale if repair work can be done soon enough. Remember that a stitch in time can save nine. Don't talk about your plans for future development too much, because anything could happen in the mean time. Better to keep silent for the time being.

Do not invest this month even though it seems like a sure thing. Wait for another chance some other time.

The health condition of the Horse will vary this month. Be on your guard against the possibility of food poisoning. Take special care when you go out hunting or diving.

Dog Month (9th October – 7th November)

Laugh and the world laughs with you

The misfortune of the Horse will be swept away by the cool autumn winds. The luck of the Horse will be as clear as the blue sky. As a matter of fact, the fortune of the Horse will be getting better and better towards the end of the year. Your daily work will be carried out smoothly without any interruption. Your relationship with your associates will be improved. You should relax and have a laugh. When you laugh, the others around you will laugh too.

The health condition of the Horse will be in good shape this month. You should bring laughter to your family so that the whole family will be full of fun. A house with a lot of laughter and joy is seldom attacked by disease.

This is going to be a month full of joy and laughter for the Horse and the people around you. And this would be a very good time for a holiday or second (or first!) honeymoon.

Pig Month (8th November – 7th December)

Silence is golden

Business will be going smoothly this month. You will receive many new orders from your clients. You will be quite successful if you are in a new partnership with people in foreign places. But one thing you have to bear in mind this month is not to be so talkative. The more you talk about other people, the more damage you will do yourself. Besides that, you should not talk too much about your future developments, especially in front of strangers. Otherwise, the success of your new developments will be seriously compromised. Try to remember that 'silence is golden'.

The Horse's finances will be pretty good. But you have to put some money by for family celebrations: weddings and birthday parties, etc.

Don't talk too much about yourself in front of your lover. Keep some things to yourself.

Mouse Month (8th December 1999 – 6th January 2000)

If a thing's worth doing, it's worth doing well

The Horse will have enough knowledge and energy to handle work easily. However, you should not be so easily satisfied. You should try your best to make use of your potential for a bigger development in the future. For the time being, you should do everything yourself, because this will be good experience for you in your future developments. Try to keep the lines of communication open to your subordinates, because you will probably get some kind of inspiration by doing so.

Finances will be at their peak of the year. You can get a good return from your investments. The purchase of properties this month will result in satisfactory profits for you. You can consider investing in starting a new business for yourself.

Show care and affections to your lover or spouse. Give him or her a gift, but choose one that's unique, to reflect your true feelings, and you should present the gift in person over a romantic dinner.

Ox Month (7th January – 4th February 2000)

The fool and his money are soon parted

Try not to be blinded by your success in the previous months. You should keep on working hard, to ensure further development in the future. You should not fool around with your associates. Without their respect, you can hardly perform your duties effectively. You should try to make use of your insight to discover the weaknesses that need to be repaired in your career. This kind of perception will help you to be more successful in the future.

Watch out for the money traps. Somebody's trying to cheat or trick you. You will lose a lot of money if you fall into these kinds of money traps. Gambling is just one example.

You will be very active in social gatherings. However, you will be disappointed if you are looking for your dream-lover.

Chapter Eight

The

Sheep

Years of the Sheep

Please keep in mind when consulting the list below that the Chinese New Year begins in early February – for example, in 1955 'the year of the Sheep' covers the period 4th February 1955 to 3rd February 1956. And if born in 1907, 1919, 1931 or 1943, the year begins on 5th February.

1907	1955
1919	1967
1931	1979
1943	1991

Distribution of the Stars within the Sign in 1999

Lucky Stars	Unlucky Stars
The Three Pillars	Bloody Knife
The Eight Chiefs	Floating Up and Down
God of Salvation	Flying Spell

Heavenly Salvation	Official Spell
	Five Ghosts
	Yellow Funeral Flag
	Decorative Top

Please refer to pages 194–213 for traditional Chinese origins of and meanings for these Stars.

General Overview of the Year

Those people born in the year of the Sheep will have a marvellous year in 1999. This is mainly due to the appearance of several Lucky Stars within the Sign. But they should keep alert since there are several Unlucky Stars in the Sign too. If not careful, their success will be spoiled at the end of the year. However, those born under this Sign should try their best to make use of the opportunities to develop their business in the first half of the year. Then they should be more conservative, in order to maintain their achievements in the second half of the year. The major concern of the Sheep this year is to try not to be involved in legal problems and to keep healthy.

Sheep will have a pretty good start to the beginning of the year. But they will be easily deceived by others, therefore they should keep their eyes wide open in the first month of the year.

Sheep will see much better achievement in their career if they are courageous enough to take the first step towards reorganizing their business or working habits during the months of the Rabbit and Dragon. They must choose the right partners to work with – don't throw pearls before swine. This will only be a waste of time and energy.

The Snake month will be one of the most unfortunate for Sheep. They should take care of their business because somebody may try to pull them down. They should try to be humble and modest in order to keep away from jealousy and troubles. They should also look after their health and watch out when it comes to road safety.

Although Sheep will be doing very well in business in the months of the Horse and Sheep, they should not be overly ambitious. They should not try to develop their business beyond their abilities. And they must prepare themselves for rainy days ahead in the autumn.

The good fortune of Sheep will carry on through the months of the Monkey and the Rooster. They will have plenty of chances for further development within these months. But they have to use a lot of effort and capital in order to earn their splendid achievements. That means they cannot get something for nothing.

There will be a 'thunderstorm' facing Sheep in the month of the Dog. They should handle their business in person, and with extreme care.

The good fortune of the Sheep will return in the Pig month. They should try to lay a solid foundation for their own future for the next year.

However, Sheep will face difficulties and troubles in the last few months of the year. They should handle business and financial matters with extreme care to ensure that they don't lose the rewards they've gained in the very last minute.

Monthly In-depth Forecasts
Tiger Month (16th February – 17th March)

You can't tell a book by its cover

Although the Sheep will have a very fortunate period of time at the beginning of the year, you must be very careful to detect enemies in hiding around you. The career of the Sheep will be badly damaged by them in the following months. Therefore, the Sheep should forget that outward appearances may be deceptive. The Sheep should examine a person through the observation of his behaviour and not by his appearance. On the contrary, if you can find some trustworthy partners to help you, you will be quite successful this year.

The Sheep's finances will be very good this month. You will make good returns from various investments. But you must keep alert and watch out for the money traps set by friends you have known for a long time.

You should keep your eyes wide open when it comes to choosing your lover. Beauty is not everything. And you cannot tell a book by its cover.

Rabbit Month (18th March – 15th April)

There is always a first time

The Sheep will see much better achievement in your career this month if you are courageous enough to take the first step in the reconstruction of your company. The original systems of your company are somewhat outdated, therefore, reforms will refresh them and bring in good income. Although there will inevitably be opposition, you should have the guts to take action at once. The Sheep may be invited to join a new project in a new place. This may be all new and strange for you, but you should give yourself a try. Don't forget that there is always a first time for everything.

The health condition of the Sheep will be in very good shape. But you should watch out for your diet and should not eat too much. Better put on more clothes to prevent a bad cold.

The Sheep will have a chance to meet others for romance. You should not be ashamed to ask for a first date, or you will miss a very good chance.

Dragon Month (16th April – 14th May)

Do not throw pearls before swine

The good fortune of the Sheep will carry on this month. You should make use of this period to develop your business diligently.

You won't be disappointed. However, the Sheep should be very careful when it comes to making choices. You must choose the right partners to work with, or all your efforts will be wasted. Your contribution is just like a pearl, and you should not throw this pearl to the swine. Besides this, you should choose the right project, or you will waste a lot of time and energy.

Although the Sheep will see a good income this month, you should not waste your money in the wrong investments. You will have luck in lottery and gambling, but try not to be too greedy.

You have to keep your eyes wide open when choosing a lover. Stop spending more time on someone who's just fooling around. Don't throw pearls to swine because it's not worthwhile.

Snake Month (15th May – 13th June)

It is easier to pull down than to build up

This will be one of the most unfortunate months for the Sheep. You should handle your business with extreme care because someone is trying to do something to destroy you. The best way for you to go forward is try to detect and to stop the conspiracy as soon as possible, because it is much easier to pull down something than to build it up. There will be some pressures coming from superiors. Try to avoid conflicts or misunderstandings. The Sheep should try not to interfere in other people's business, or there will be a lot of troubles in the following months.

The health condition of the Sheep will not be so good this month. You must watch out for your safety in water. Be more cautious in swimming, diving and fishing.

There will be troubles between the Sheep and your lover this month. You must be patient. Calm down your temper to avoid a serious conflict.

Horse Month (14th June – 12th July)

You can't win them all

This month will be the calm after the storm. The working condition and development of the Sheep will be on an upward trend again. The Sheep will be involved in more and more projects. However, you should not be too ambitious about finishing all your jobs within a short period of time. As long as you can see good development in several important projects, the Sheep should not care too much about the others. It's as simple as the saying that goes, 'you can't win them all'. The major concern of the Sheep in this month is to try to focus only on the important matters. 'Diversity' will only lead to a mess.

The Sheep will have a good income this month. But there will be a lot of expenses too. You will end up with nothing gained if you don't mind your budget.

The Sheep will be very busily engaged in social activities, and you will be very popular. But you should not spend too much time in the pursuit of love affairs.

Sheep Month (13th July – 10th August)

You don't get something for nothing

There will be some obstacles facing the Sheep this month. You must put more effort into your career, or this will become an unproductive month. Besides that, the Sheep may have to put in more money for the development of the business. That means more effort and more money are needed for the Sheep to gain a satisfactory result. You don't get something for nothing. It would be a big help if you can find a reliable ally. This would a big help for you at the year end.

Finances will drop down a little bit this month. It would be better if you can save more money to re-invest in your business.

The health condition of the Sheep will not be so good this month, especially in the first week of the month. You should pay more attention to your diet and hygiene, at home and when away from home.

Monkey Month (11th August – 9th September)

Wonders will never cease

This will be one of the most fortunate months for the Sheep in business. You can uncover 'wonders' this month if you work hard enough. You will find that chances come one after another. You should not let these chances slip away, because they will never return. Build up your confidence by exploring new possibilities for your business this month. You will be amazed by the response if you dare to make a request from authority. You may hear good news about overseas developments at the beginning of the month.

Finances will be on an upward trend again this month. You will get very good returns from your investments. This is a good time to purchase a car and/or home.

The Sheep should not be shy about looking out for a new lover. And you will receive a welcome surprise in love matters in the middle of the month.

Rooster Month (10th September – 8th October)

What goes up, must come down

The good fortune of the Sheep in the previous three months will drop down this month. It's just like the old saying, 'what goes up must come down'. Fortunately, you can still run your business without too many troubles. But you will find out that there will be fewer and fewer chances for you in this month. What you should do is concentrate on your present objectives and projects and forget about any new developments. You should keep on looking for reliable partners if you could not find any last month.

The health condition of the Sheep will be in bad shape this month. You will suffer from various aches. And you will have problems sleeping. Things would be much better if you could take a relaxing holiday.

Relations between you and your lover or spouse will be at a low ebb. This means you should handle the situation with care and patience. You'd better walk away for a while before you lose control in front of him or her.

Dog Month (9th October – 7th November)

When the cat's away, the mice will play

This will be one of the most unfortunate months for the Sheep this year. You should be careful about handling your business within this period of time, because anything could happened. You should try to spend more time looking after your business in person. Don't depend on others to do this for you. Your business will be messed up during your absence. Remember that 'when the cat's away, the mice will play'. If possible, go to your branch offices to supervise their business as well. Orders and products will therefore be sharply increased.

Finances will be at their lowest ebb of the year. Be more conservative with your money. Keep out thieves and burglars by locking your windows and doors securely, and watch your pockets.

The health condition of the Sheep will be in very bad shape. You will have problems with your respiratory or digestive system. Better go to see the doctor for proper treatment.

Pig Month (8th November – 7th December)

Good seed makes a good crop

This will be a much better month than last month. You should try to make use of this period of time to develop your business for the future. Good planning for the future will be like planting good seeds in the soil. There will be a good harvest later on. Try to contact your clients in person in order to develop your business in the future. Besides this, the Sheep should show your subordinates that you care, because their support will be a solid foundation for the success of your business.

The Sheep's finances will be much improved this month. You will have good fortune in investments and lotteries. But be careful because your luck will suddenly disappear near the end of the month.

This will be a very romantic month for the Sheep. Your little attentions and kindnesses towards your beloved will win you his or her true love. But you should not spend too much in love affairs. Business before pleasure.

Mouse Month (8th December 1999 – 6th January 2000)

Bad news travels fast

There will be a lot of difficulties and troubles facing the Sheep this month. You should handle your business with patience. Try to solve these one by one in order not to mess up the whole thing. There will be a lot of rumours about you. You should try to find out the source of these and try to stop them as soon as possible because 'bad news travels fast'. If they cannot be stopped in time, then your reputation will be badly damaged. The Sheep should watch out for the quality of your products. Otherwise, a lot of complaints and criticism will arise.

The Sheep's finances drop down sharply this month. No luck in investments and gambling. Make sure that you have paid all bills, or you will see losses sooner or later.

The Sheep should not be talkative this month. The more you talk, the less attractive you will be among your friends and lovers.

Ox Month (7th January – 4th February 2000)

Every cloud has a silver lining

The Sheep should not be frustrated with the problems faced last month. Don't forget that 'every cloud has a silver lining'. You will receive some comfort this month. The obstacles in front of you will dissolve gradually and your fortune will be getting better and better towards the end of the year. Your efforts and contributions will be deeply appreciated. There will be a promotion for the Sheep at the beginning of next year if you work hard enough. But you will still be bothered by rumours and criticisms. You have to stand firm for the protection of your own reputation and rights.

The health of the Sheep will be in bad shape this month. You will become the victim of infections if you cannot take care of yourself properly. Watch the food you eat, especially if venturing to foreign countries.

The Sheep will feel rather uneasy about love affairs this month because relations with your lover will fluctuate within this period of time. The best way forward is to communicate with sincerity and patience, and try to reach a mutual understanding.

Chapter Nine

The

Monkey

Years of the Monkey

Please keep in mind when consulting the list below that the Chinese New Year begins in early February – for example, in 1956 'the year of the Monkey' covers the period 5th February 1956 to 3rd February 1957. The exception to this is for those born in 1992, when the year begins on 4th February. See chart page xv.

1908	1956
1920	1968
1932	1980
1944	1992

Distribution of the Stars within the Sign in 1999

Lucky Stars	Unlucky Stars
Lunar Virtue	Deadly Spell
Earthly Salvation	Gradual Drain
	Threat of Robbery

Please refer to pages 194–213 for traditional Chinese origins of and meanings for these Stars.

General Overview of the Year

Those people who were born in the year of the Monkey will have a rough year in 1999. This is mainly due to the appearance of three Unlucky Stars within the Sign. Fortunately, Monkeys will have much better luck in the second half of the year, so they should persevere until the last minute for the final victory. They should show more care towards the people around them; this will bring a good return. The major concern for Monkeys in 1999 is to keep a careful eye on their health and safety. It's a wise idea to go for a medical check-up as soon as possible and to receive proper treatment if anything should go wrong.

Monkeys will not have a good start to the beginning of the year. There will be a lot of difficulties facing them in business in the first three months. They should handle their business with patience. Think before you climb – a hasty climb will lead to a big fall.

However, Monkeys will enjoy a fortunate period of time in the months of the Snake and Horse. Not only will their business greatly improve, but also their fortune and health will be in much better shape during this period of time. They will have a wonderful holiday during this time. And they will be refreshed and inspired by the trip.

The months of the Sheep and Monkey will be the most difficult for Monkeys. They should use their intelligence to find their way out of their problems. It would be a big help if they can find a reliable ally during these struggles.

The obstacles facing Monkeys will be removed in the months of the Rooster and Dog. They will have a very successful and productive period of time within these months if they can equip themselves with more knowledge and strong determination.

When Monkeys face problems, it is best to keep an open mind and accept different opinions from different kinds of people. Besides this, they should try to avoid a total collapse physically during the month of the Dog.

Fortunately, the Monkey will have much better luck in the last two months of the year. They will have a good harvest at the year end. But they should try to develop business according to their abilities, and no further. Beware of over-expansion.

Monthly In-depth Forecasts
Tiger Month (16th February – 17th March)

Soon ripe, soon rotten

Monkeys will not have a good start to the beginning of the year. They will face problems both in business and in health. Therefore, they should pay more attention to their day-to-day work. Otherwise, there will be a mess in their business. Their business development seems to be the most outstanding feature right now, but it can all go sour suddenly. So the prime concern for Monkeys this month is to keep the momentum going in business and to avoid a sudden decline. The best way forward is to keep a careful eye on service and production control, especially near the end the month.

Finances will be at a low ebb, so you'd be best off not expecting too much. You will lose money if you make any investments or indulge in any gambling.

Love will be very unstable this month. Relations between you and your lover may witness a dramatic change, so you should be very careful in the way you handle this fragile relationship during this sensitive period of time.

Rabbit Month (18th March – 15th April)

Better to wear out than to rust away

You tend to skip away from your duties this month. The heavy workload and continuous pressure make you frustrated and looking for an escape route. Under this situation, a short rest will be all right, but to quit for long will badly hurt your future. Everybody has to stand firm in the face of difficulties if they want to achieve success. Those who cannot persist up to the last minute will never succeed. Don't forget that it is better to wear out than to rust away.

The Monkey's finances will see a little improvement this month. However, it's still not the right time for investments and gambling. You will have better luck in the second half of the year – wait until then.

Health will be in good shape this month. But you should take care the health of elder family members. Make sure they will get the proper medical treatment as soon as possible.

Dragon Month (16th April – 14th May)

Hasty climbers have sudden falls

Prepare yourself well before you attempt a climb up to the higher ground. You have to think before you climb. Otherwise, you may find that the fruits on top of the trees are all rotten. And you may have a big fall. Therefore, think it over carefully before you take any chance. What you should do this month is enrich your knowledge and wait for the right time, which is coming in the months that follow.

Watch out for your safety when engaged in outdoor activities, such as camping and hunting. Keep away from the edges of steep slopes. Keep alert, and don't get lost in the wilderness.

Try not to make a hasty decision regarding love or marriage. You may live to be very sorry in future.

Snake Month (15th May – 13th June)

A rising tide lifts all boats

After having three unfortunate months at the beginning of the year, Monkeys will have much better luck over the next two. Your fortune changes from bad to good. As the old saying goes, 'a rising tide lifts all boats'. All the obstacles facing the Monkey will be dissolved at once this month. This enables you to walk fast and steadily on your way to success. There is the chances of promotion if you work hard enough.

Your finances will be very good this month. You will be a lucky winner in the lottery. And you will realize additional income. Don't forget to give a helping hand to those who need it.

You will be energetic this month. But you must observe caution about the food you eat when you are away from home.

Horse Month (14th June – 12th July)

Travel broadens the mind

You will see satisfactory achievement in your business this month if you work hard enough. However, you should try to find some leisure time for yourself. A holiday will not only refresh your mind, but can also inspire your creativity too. You should travel with your eyes open to observe, and your ears open to listen. This means you should try to learn as much from your travels to foreign countries as possible. But watch out for dangers and try to keep away from them during your travels.

Finances will drop a bit, but there's nothing you should worry about. But you have to save money to prepare for enormous and unexpected expenses in the coming two months.

The Monkey will be very popular in social activities. However, you should try not to talk about politics or religion too much, or there will be a lot of troubles aroused.

Sheep Month (13th July – 10th August)

Of two evils, choose the lesser

There will be a lot of difficulties facing the Monkey this month. You will face a very complicated relationship in your career. It would be much better if you can keep neutral. If not, then you have to make a choice. Remember the old saying, 'of two evils choose the lesser'. This tactic can also apply to the day-to-day grind. If there are two unprofitable projects to choose from, you should opt for the one that stands to lose less money. You have to make many different choices this month. Your success this year will depend chiefly on these choices.

The Monkey's finances will be very poor this month. You will lose money in your investments. You must know how to make the right choices among them.

The mood of the Monkey will be going up and down. And you will be emotional and difficult to deal with. You should try to calm down and not scare your friends and lover away.

Monkey Month (11th August – 9th September)

Faith will move mountains

The bad luck of the Monkey will come like a summer thunderstorm. The damage will be quite serious if the Monkey doesn't prepare well in advance. You will face strong challenges and economic crises. You have to stand firm, with a strong determination and belief in your ability to survive. You should have faith in yourself and your associates as well. Don't forget that 'Faith will move mountains.' The Monkey should concentrate on only one major project, and not try to jumble a lot of things together. Don't give up even in the most critical moments because your luck will be improving in the second half of the year.

Finances will see no improvement at all in this month. You have to watch your expenses carefully. Make sure that all your bills can be paid on time.

You will be suspicious in your personal life. You should have faith in your lover or spouse.

Rooster Month (10th September – 8th October)

Knowledge is power

This is one of the most fortunate months for the Monkey this year. You will have the chance to prove your ability. However, you should enrich your power through self-knowledge. This will enable you to have much better bargaining power than your competitors. Don't forget that 'knowledge is power'. The Monkey will be invited to join several joint-ventures this month. You should choose only one of these to try. The result will be quite satisfactory if you have made the right choice. This month will the right time for the Monkey to start a new page in your career.

The Monkey will have the necessary perceptiveness to tell which investment is worthwhile. Therefore, you will see a good return. You will have luck in lotteries and gambling.

The health condition of the Monkey will be in pretty good shape this month. But you should watch out when it comes to road safety. Drive with special care in the first week of the month.

Dog Month (9th October – 7th November)

It takes all sorts to make a world

Try to broaden your business connections this month. You should try to approach your clients and the related financial backing with sincerity. This will help you to realize much better development in the future. You should be open-minded about accepting different kinds of people in your company because it takes all sorts of people to make a world. Different opinions from different kinds of people will lead to a splendid outcome. The Monkey should put by some money for a rainy day – one's coming next month.

The health condition of the Monkey will be pretty weak this month. You should try to get enough rest, and don't run yourself ragged with continuous hard work. Get a proper medical check up to make sure that everything is all right.

The Monkey should be more flexible towards your love affairs. You should accept the weakness of your lover if you really love him or her. Don't forget that nobody is perfect.

Pig Month (8th November – 7th December)

Ask no questions and hear no lies

Complicated personal inter-relationships will produce a lot of uncertainty this month. You will become the hapless victim in these disputes if you don't know how to handle this situation. The best way for you to survive is ask no questions and hear no lies. You should mind your own business and ignore the rumours and gossip about other people. Besides this, you should not forget to perform your duty effectively. You should try not to put in place any major changes in your business this month.

You will lose a lot of money if you risk it in investments and gambling. You should lock up the windows and doors of your house securely to keep the burglars at bay. And try not to walk along dark streets alone at night.

Trust your lover or spouse. Ask no questions and hear no lies. Everything will clear up soon.

Mouse Month (8th December 1999 – 6th January 2000)

God helps those who help themselves

The Monkey will have a very heavy workload this month; try to finish it on your own and as soon as possible. You should not rely on other people to complete the whole job for you. Besides that, you have to find the way out for yourself. Remember that 'God helps those who help themselves'. The Monkey will then reap a very good harvest at year end.

The Monkey's finances will be improved a little bit this month, but still won't be good enough to make a good income for you. Don't expect too much. You will have some unexpected bills at the beginning of the month.

Ox Month (7th January – 4th February 2000)

Stretch no further than your arms will reach

This is one of the most favourable months for the Monkey of this year. You should try to make use of this period of time to expand your business. But you should not go too far. You should make the expansion according to your ability. Over-expansion will bring a total collapse. Your efforts and skills will be appreciated by your superiors. And you will get the merit that you deserve at the end of the year.

Finances will be at their peak of the year. You will receive a handsome bonus. Besides that, you will get good returns from your various investments.

This will not be a romantic month for the Monkey. You have the feeling of being deserted even though you are surrounded by friends and family members.

Chapter Ten

The

Rooster

Years of the Rooster

Please keep in mind when consulting the list below that the Chinese New Year begins in early February – for example, in 1957 'the year of the Rooster' covers the period 4th February 1957 to 3rd February 1958.

1909	1957
1921	1969
1933	1981
1945	1993

Distribution of the Stars within the Sign for 1999

Lucky Star	Unlucky Stars
God of Study and Career	Broken Down
	Conflict of the Year
	Huge Drain
	Iron Bars
	Gaol House

Please refer to pages 194–213 for traditional Chinese origins of and meanings for these Stars.

General Overview of the Year

1999 will be a very exciting, somewhat turbulent, year for Roosters. They will be inspired, creative and driven by ambition. It is this drive that will be met by objections. Finances must be scrupulously managed. Pay attention to spending, and make sure all investments are affordable, otherwise there could be a shortage of funds. In business make sure all undertakings are well within the scope of the law – legal irregularities could lead to conviction.

The first two months of the year will be financially good, but resist the influence of less than savoury friends, as this could be detrimental. Don't gamble.

The months of the Dragon and the Snake will be filled with inspiration and bring much better luck. Be modest – any sign of arrogance could meet with severe opposition.

The months of the Horse and Sheep will be challenging for the Rooster. This is a time for efficiency and attention to detail. Double-check all legal documents and contracts; this will alleviate legal problems later. Heights should be treated with respect, so take care if you should be mountaineering or on steep inclines.

The months of the Monkey and Rooster will see improvement. The combination of creativity and hard work will receive recognition, and this will give the Rooster additional bargaining power.

There will be conflicts of interest in the month of the Dog, so swallow your pride and be more tolerant.

The months of the Pig and Mouse are another good period. Concentrate on the job at hand and don't over-indulge, particularly in alcohol or drugs.

The Rooster will have a lot of problems in the last month of the year. Manage financial matters cautiously and diversify your investments.

Monthly In-depth Forecasts
Tiger Month (16th February – 17th March)

A bird never flew on one wing

The Rooster will face many difficulties at the start of the year. With the help and support of family, friends and work colleagues the Rooster will overcome these difficulties smoothly and successfully. If you try to go it alone you will be like a bird with only one wing – like this bird, sooner or later you will fall from the sky. It will be a busy time, especially at the end of the month. Pay attention to detail, particularly in the work environment, or there could be careless and expensive mistakes. This is not the month to change jobs.

The Rooster will be very lucky in financial matters, and will show an excellent return on financial investments. This luck will change at the end of the month when the Rooster will need to exercise caution in putting financial success on display. In order to avoid a robbery refrain from wearing too much jewellery or flashing money around.

Rabbit Month (18th March – 15th April)

The bigger they are the harder they fall.

This month you will need to be very careful in how you handle your relationships in order to avoid being isolated. Never before has the Rooster needed family and colleagues more; their support is vital in avoiding a big fall, like a giant rock rolling all the way down from the top of the hill to the bottom. Don't be too arrogant – instead, try showing some consideration towards others.

Financially the Rooster is in decline this month. My advice is to be more conservative when investing, as there is a likelihood of losing money, and avoid seeking a loan, as this will result in endless trouble.

Whilst the Rooster will have many friends around this month it is difficult to find even one person with whom to share innermost feelings, or confide in.

Don't expect too much from your love life, there will not be too much progress in this area. Next month is looking better.

Dragon Month (16th April – 14th May)

One good turn deserves another

Remember all those who have offered support and friendship in the past. Their continued support is a key factor in future developments. Seek the advice and guidance of superiors, as their help is likely to mean even more progress. This is a splendid month of achievements for the Rooster, and this upward trend should continue unabated. The Rooster will be deeply appreciated and will become deservedly famous.

Finances are improving, however you will have a lot of expenses and could end up empty-handed if you are not careful with your cash. Notwithstanding this fact, this is an excellent time to purchase a small delicate gift for a loved one. This gesture will be greatly rewarded.

The health of the Rooster is much better than it has been in the last couple of months. You will be feeling strong and energetic, consequently this is a good time to communicate with friends and clients alike.

Snake Month (15th May – 13th June)

The early bird catches the worm

Competition is tough this month. The trick is to act quickly. Speedy action plus hard work and determination will secure a lead over the Rooster's opponents. Make sure that your attention is completely focused on important issues, as distractions could result in missed opportunities. Partnership is important, but make sure the partner selected is dependable – this will avert a possible casualty in the near future.

To ensure a productive year, it would be wise for the Rooster to formulate a plan and put it into action this month. This is an excellent month for starting a new business, or for investing. Gambling is definitely out of the question, especially at the end of the month, as the Rooster's luck will be up and down like a roller coaster.

Follow a good health plan this month, keep a balanced diet, exercise and get enough sleep. If hiking is planned this month then make sure to avoid heights – the Rooster could have an accidental fall. Keep away from dangerous precipices and steep steps.

Horse Month (14th June – 12th July)

Old habits die hard

There could be a sharp fall on the career ladder for the Rooster. Take care to prevent the situation from declining even further. In order to survive in the workplace the Rooster will need to be inventive in order to create a breakthrough – conventional measures are not likely to succeed. Try taking the advice of a colleague, as a headstrong attitude will only lead to failure.

The health of the Rooster is fine this month. Try getting rid of all those bad habits like smoking and excessive drinking, as these will badly damage the Rooster's health long term.

Roosters will appear very cool and unfriendly this month. Don't forget to smile, particularly in social gatherings. Remember, 'it is better to have more friends than enemies'.

Sheep Month (13th July – 10th August)

The darkest hour is just before dawn

Last month and this will be the darkest months for the Rooster this year. You will face a lot of trouble and conflict at work. Don't be too trusting of colleagues because they are exploring every opportunity to make a sudden attack, which could be fatal. The attacks will come from within and the Rooster will be the victim. You must make every effort to protect yourself in this troubled period. This is not a good time to make a career change, it could lead to a fatal blow in the near future. The financial situation is very poor for the Rooster this month. There will be unexpected expenses that could cause financial problems. All bills should be settled promptly, as late payment could present problems.

Relationships, too, will be poor this month. There will be friction amongst friends and emotions could run high. The Rooster should try to remain calm and cheerful at this critical time – the darkest hour is just before dawn. Remember the morning sun will rise soon.

Monkey Month (11th August – 9th September)

Fine feathers make fine birds

Choose friends and partners carefully. These people will have a strong influence over the well-being of the Rooster this month, it is even possible that a group of sinister or corrupt friends could ruin the public image and damage the business of the Rooster.

It is time for the Rooster to pay attention to appearances; judgements will be made on presentation, both personal presentation and presentation of work. This will greatly improve the likelihood of success. Don't mess things up half-way.

Finances are improving this month. Short-term investments will be beneficial. If long-term investment is being contemplated, wait until November.

Your social calendar is busy this month. Remember public image is important, so dress appropriately for the occasion.

Rooster Month (10th September – 8th October)

If you can't beat 'em, join 'em

The challenges which the Rooster faces this month will be too strong to overcome.

This is the time for diplomacy and skilful strategy – basically, try reaching a compromise with your opponents, if not necessarily an agreement: 'If you can't beat 'em, join 'em.' This action will release you from pressure and allow you to delegate difficult tasks to your rivals. However the Rooster should take care to follow all rules and regulations or you could well face legal hassles.

The Rooster is regaining lost energy levels and strength this month. Don't ruin this by eating badly or taking unnecessary pills or drugs.

The tension between you and your partner or spouse will gradually begin to dissolve. If single, the Rooster could fall in love this month, but beware the sweet and smooth one.

Dog Month (9th October – 7th November)

Better safe than sorry

In many ways this is a dangerous month for the Rooster. In business the Rooster faces serious tests. If these are not handled carefully and properly it will mean total defeat. Be conservative and play it safe, especially in the first two weeks. Tread carefully, step by step, and watch out for traps.

Be alert to those around you, as someone who appears to be sympathetic could be an impostor. Don't commit to any financial matters, especially in the middle of the month.

The Rooster could be quite emotional this month. Try to remain calm, especially with your partner or spouse. Don't provoke him or her, as this could result in the relationship being broken off.

Pig Month (8th November – 7th December)

Honesty is the best policy

The most simple and effective way for the Rooster to win support from others is through honesty. Open up and discuss ideas directly with those involved. Don't try to cover up or cheat – exposing your weaknesses will not only allow personal growth but could be a successful business tactic.

The finances of the Rooster will be much improved this month. You will have an increase in income, could win the lottery, and will make a good return through buying or selling property.

Tension is released in personal relationships. Be polite and honest to a new friend. Old friends will visit from overseas.

Mouse Month (8th December 1999 – 6th January 2000)

You never miss the water till the well runs dry

The Rooster should show gratitude to colleagues or friends and not take them for granted. Recognize and acknowledge the support which they have given in the past, for if they withdraw their help in the future the Rooster will be in deep trouble. Consolidate your relationship with old partners, don't discard old for new, as this will lead to regret.

The Rooster should cut all unnecessary expenses this month as you could lose much in the middle of the month. Try to save money as one would save water during a drought, or the water will be missed when the well runs dry. It would be wise to conserve as much energy as possible this month. Refrain from bad habits and over-indulging, as a total collapse could result from burning the candle at both ends.

Ox Month (7th January – 4th February 2000)

Don't put all your eggs in one basket

This has not been a good year for Roosters. There have been many difficulties and challenges throughout the year which the Rooster has had to overcome. Not even in the last month will the Rooster be allowed to relax – if you do you could lose everything at the very last moment. Modesty will be the best way to avoid becoming the prime target and to survive conflicts.

It is a good time to diversify investments. Don't invest everything in a single project. The basket of eggs will fall and everything in it will be lost.

This could be a dull period for the Rooster – even finding a companion to share a happy moment will prove difficult. Perhaps you should reconsider your relationship with former partners, and make an effort to be more affectionate.

Chapter Eleven

The
Dog

Years of the Dog

Please keep in mind when consulting the list below that the Chinese New Year begins in early February – for example, in 1958 'the year of the Dog' covers the period 4th February 1958 to 3rd February 1959. The exception to this is 1910 – see chart page xv.

1910	1958
1922	1970
1934	1982
1946	1994

Distribution of the Stars within the Sign in 1999

Lucky Stars	Unlucky Stars
Dragon's Virtue	Heavenly Threat
Crape Myrtle	Heavenly Hazards
Jade Hall	Yearly Threat
Union of the Year	Swallowed Up
	Sudden Collapse

Please refer to pages 194–213 for traditional Chinese origins of and meanings for these Stars.

General Overview of the Year

Those people born in the year of the Dog will have a very success-ful and productive year in 1999. This is mainly due to the appear-ance of several Lucky Stars within the Sign. Although several Unlucky Stars appear as well, their negative effects will be mini-mized and neutralized by the Lucky Stars, and therefore will cause no serious harm.

Dogs' business development will be pretty smooth, and they will have strong support from their superiors. The only thing they have to worry about is how to keep their rewards after long strug-gles. They should watch out for sudden financial collapse.

Dogs will see a very fortunate start to the year. They should try to lay down a solid foundation for the future development in the first two months. They will face fewest difficulties if they start their new projects within these two months.

But the luck of the Dog will drop sharply in the month of the Dragon. They should handle their work with patience and try to keep a low profile to avoid suspicion and jealousy. They should not try to take medicines without the consent and advice of their GP.

Fortunately, the luck of Dogs will change from bad to good in the months of the Snake, Horse and Sheep. They should carry on their business step by step, and perform their duty by themselves. Although their fortune will be pretty good within this period of time, they should avoid potential money traps.

The working progress of Dogs will be rather sluggish in the months of the Monkey and Rooster. However, they should not give up because there will be an important breakthrough at the end of the year. They should persist to the last minute. They should keep their eyes wide open to detect any cheating and conspiracy around them. They should not risk their money in investment and gambling to avoid an economic crisis.

The month of the Pig will be the most unfortunate period of time for the Dog. They should try their best to handle their business and finances. They should try to settle controversies and conflicts within their family. Better to put out a small fire before it becomes a conflagration. Besides that, they should not let 'the last drop make the cup run over'.

Fortunately, Dogs can relax with satisfactory rewards after their year-long struggle. The problems in business and finance will all disappear in the last two months of the year. This will be a very favourable period of time for Dogs to turn a new page in business. And, most important of all, they will enjoy a sweet family life within these two months.

Monthly In-depth Forecasts
Tiger Month (16th February – 17th March)

A good beginning makes a good ending

The Dog will have a very good start to the beginning of the year. You should work very hard like the farmer, putting good seed into the soil in the early spring. If you can make use of this favourable period of time, then you are going to have a good harvest at year end. Don't let the chance slip away through your fingers in this month. Otherwise, it won't be a productive year for you. You should go out to find opportunities, like the early birds in the early spring looking for food. You will see a very good return by doing so.

The fortune of the Dog will be very prosperous this month. You will receive unexpected income. Your luck in investments and lotteries will be very good within this period of time.

The Dog will have a good beginning with your new love. You will turn a new page in your love affairs. You should take care of it as you would look after the new bud of a beautiful rose.

Rabbit Month (18th March – 15th April)

Good things come in small packages

The Dog will have a very fortunate period of time in the first two months of the year. Your work will be carried out smoothly without any interruption. You will be promoted if you work hard enough. And there will be some good news about your business from overseas. Besides this, relations with your superiors and associates will be greatly improved, so that you won't be bothered by internal disputes any more. The sum of all these benefits will provide a very good basis for future development in business.

Although there will not be a handsome income for the Dog this month, small bonuses will add up to a pretty good fortune. However, you should try to cut down on unnecessary expenses.

You will receive gifts from your lover or spouse. This is a very important message from them to you. Therefore, you should not overlook this message.

Dragon Month (16th April – 14th May)

A little knowledge is a dangerous thing

You will face a series of difficulties in your business this month. You should try to handle these with patience. Besides this, you should keep a low profile in order to keep away from suspicion and jealousy. Otherwise the situation could get even worse. Most important of all is that you should keep silent about things you don't know too much about. Don't expose your weaknesses publicly. Listen to professional advice. The best way forward this month is to try to gain more knowledge about your business.

You should not invest money in projects that you are not familiar with, or you will lose a lot of money.

Your health will be in bad shape this month. Take care of yourself, especially when away from home. Don't try to self-medicate; always seek the advice of your GP.

Snake Month (15th May – 13th June)

Second thoughts are best

The Dog will be emotional this month. Therefore, you should try to calm yourself when dealing with business matters. You have to reconsider the whole thing carefully again and again before you make any important decision. If possible, ask others for their opinion. Beware that your intuition may deceive you. Keep in mind that 'second thoughts are best'. You should not let your speech run faster than your thoughts. The prime concern for the Dog in this month is to keep calm and silent.

Your health will see a little improvement, but you still have to take care of yourself. Take special care of your digestive system.

Do not make any important decisions regarding marriage, or you will live to regret them. Mind your words in front of your lover or spouse.

Horse Month (14th June – 12th July)

If you want something done well, do it yourself

The fortune of the Dog will take an upward turn this month. Your business will be running smoothly. However, if you want to realize even better achievements, you should take on more yourself, especially when it comes to financial matters. You can ask others to assist you in running your business, but do not rely on them totally – not only because you will be cheated, but also because the entire business will be put in jeopardy. Remember the old saying: 'If you want something done well, do it yourself.'

The fortune of the Dog will be pretty good this month. Remember, however, to handle financial matters by yourself. Somebody may try to cheat you.

Express your affection to your lover or spouse in a direct way. Don't be ashamed or reluctant to say sorry for previous wrong-doing.

Sheep Month (13th July – 10th August)

Rome wasn't built in a day

The Dog will be ambitious this month. You try to finish all your tasks in the shortest amount of time. But this will lead to ever more onerous burdens. Complete work steadily, to avoid mistakes. The prime concern for the Dog in this month is to try to work with patience. Don't forget that 'Rome was not built in a day'. Beware of over-expansion, too. Try to perform your duties according to your abilities, and no further.

The fortune of the Dog will decline a bit this month. You should spare some money for unexpected bills and expenses in the coming four months.

The Dog should try to approach a new lover with patience. Persist even if you have been rejected before. Don't forget: 'Faith moves mountains.'

Monkey Month (11th August – 9th September)

He who rides a tiger is afraid to dismount

Never push too hard when you are dealing with associates and clients this month – especially when you are making use of the authority of your superiors. Otherwise, you will have nowhere to turn if anything goes wrong. The main concern for the Dog in this month is to build good relations with those around you, or you will become like, as the proverb says, 'he who rides a tiger' – afraid to dismount. To be humble and modest is the best way to go this month.

Health will not pose many problems, but mind your safety in forests and mountains. Try to keep away from wild animals and steep slopes.

Be nice and gentle towards friends and family members this month. Violence will only lead to broken relationships.

Rooster Month (10th September – 8th October)

A live dog is better than a dead lion

The Dog will face a very heavy workload again this month. You should try to meet your deadlines on time, but don't exhaust yourself in the process. The prime concern for the Dog this month is how to meet the demands of work and your own needs, without any conflicts. You will have to choose a competent partner or ally, but this won't be easy. A person's future potential, not current performance, is the most important factor in this matter. Don't forget that 'a live dog is much better than a dead lion'.

Finances will be improved a little bit, yet you should not try your luck in investments or gambling.

Pay special attention to your health. You should try your best to avoid total burnout. It's not worthwhile ruining your health in the pursuit of work.

Dog Month (9th October – 7th November)

No smoke without fire

There will be something very unusual taking place in business this month. Keep your eyes wide open. Where there's smoke, there's fire. Find the fire and put it out at the earliest possible time. In other words, try to root out any conspiracies or cheating taking place around you. This month is definitely not a good time to start a new joint venture. In addition, be very careful when it comes to handling legal matters.

There will be several unexpected bills this month. You will be left in embarrassing economic circumstances if you don't handle your money wisely and carefully.

Try to settle quarrels and disputes with your lover or spouse. Better to put out a small fire before it becomes a raging inferno.

Pig Month (8th November – 7th December)

The last drop makes the cup run over

This will be one of the most unfortunate months for the Dog this year. You have been under the pressure of a heavy workload and continuous problems for several months. However, you should persevere to the last minute and should not give up. Your luck will take an upward turn in the next two months. The problem is that in the mean time you will face serious tests. If you don't stand firm, you will be beaten flat. It's always that last drop of water that makes the cup run over. The prime concern of the Dog this month is not to give up in any case.

Financially the Dog cannot be optimistic this month. You should watch your expenses. Beware of unexpected bills that come at the last minute.

Your health will be all right this month, but keep an eye on the health of younger family members. Keep all medicines and sharp objects out of their reach.

Mouse Mouth (8th December 1999 – 6th January 2000)

After a storm comes a calm

The Dog can relax a little bit after your hard slog in previous months. Your heavy workload will be greatly reduced and the obstacles in front of you will gradually be removed. This month sees the calm after the storm. Take this time to repair and to re-adjust yourself, just as a captain repairs the damage to his ship and then re-sets his course. You will reach your destination at year end by doing so. This is also a good time to broaden your business con-nections and to improve relations with associates.

Mind your health, particularly when it comes to your diet. If you don't you will leave yourself open to diarrhoea and other infections. Don't forget to put on extra layers of clothing to protect from the cold.

The Dog will enjoy a peaceful and sweet personal life this month. This would be a wonderful time for you to go on holiday with your loved one.

Ox Month (7th January – 4th February 2000)

East, west, home's best

This will be one of the most fortunate months for the Dog this year. You will be making good progress at work and will have nothing to worry about. You will be invited to take part in some new projects. And this month is a suitable time to initiate new developments in business. Relations with superiors and associates will also see improvement. Besides this, you will get the necessary economic support for your business. This means you won't have to worry about capital.

Your health will also see improvements this month. However, you should maintain a regular schedule for your daily life. Keep in mind that you'd better not eat or drink too much over the holidays.

The Dog will enjoy a very sweet family life this month. There will be a chance of reconciliation with family members whom you haven't been in touch with for a long while.

狗

Chapter Twelve

猪

The

Pig

Years of the Pig

Please keep in mind when consulting the list below that the Chinese New Year begins in early February – for example, in 1959 'the year of the Pig' covers the period 4th February 1959 to 3rd February 1960. The exceptions to this are the years 1911, 1923 and 1935 – see chart page xv.

1911	1959
1923	1971
1935	1983
1947	1995

Distribution of the Stars within the Sign in 1999

Lucky Stars   Unlucky Stars

Lucky Stars	Unlucky Stars
None	Pointing at the Back
	White Tiger
	Fierce Hercules
	Earthly Threat

Please refer to pages 194–213 for traditional Chinese origins of and meanings for these Stars.

General Overview of the Year

Those people born in the year of the Pig will have a year full of challenges and conflicts in 1999. There are no Lucky Stars at all within the Sign, so Pigs will have no one but themselves to depend on in their year-long struggle. Pigs will hear a lot of rumours and criticisms, and some picky people will be watching them very closely. Therefore, they should behave themselves at all times. In addition, they must keep safety uppermost in mind when taking part in outdoor activities. Nor can they expect too much in terms of financial growth. In all probability there may be negative cash flow between Spring and Summer if they don't take care of their money properly.

Having said this, Pigs will see a pretty good start to the year. Their work will be carried out smoothly without any interruptions. They will do even better in the month of the Rabbit. But they must have the guts to take calculated risks. They will get a good return on their investments if they do.

The months of the Dragon and Snake will not be a favourable period for Pigs to develop their business. They will tend to find many excuses for facing up to difficulties – but this will only make the situation even worse. They should face up to reality and try to solve the difficulties practically. They should also cut down on the number of projects they have on the go at once.

Fortunately, luck will be on an upward trend in the months of the Horse and Sheep. Business will be carried out successfully if Pigs can find a reliable partner. There will be new stimulation for the business development of Pigs within this period of time. But they should not forget to keep away from so-called friends who actually mean them harm.

Bad luck will come suddenly with the thunderstorms of the months of the Monkey and Rooster. Pigs should take their business seriously, and never try to fool around at work or in matters of the heart. If they play with fire, they will get burned.

Although the luck of the Pigs will be improved a little bit during this time, it will still not be good enough for them to develop new projects. This will be the time to forget about the unhappy experiences of the past few months, yet remain modest and unassuming in all things.

Efforts and contributions in the past will be deeply appreciated. Pigs will become the focus of interest at social gatherings. However, they should prepare themselves for the chaos that could erupt at the end of the year.

Pigs will face strong challenges and oppositions in the last month of the year. In addition, they may have to face the loss of a loved one. They must try to bear in mind that pain and trial by fire will help them to become more mature.

Monthly In-depth Forecasts
Tiger Month (16th February – 17th March)

When in Rome do as the Romans do

The Pig will have a moderate period of time at the beginning of the year. This means your work will be carried out as usual without any interruptions, though without any breakthroughs either. Your prime concern this month will be not to become isolated from the majority. You should try to be more flexible, and do as the Romans do. You will win the necessary support by doing so. Otherwise, you will be rejected and excluded by your associates and clients, and that will bring a lot of problems in the months to come.

The Pig should not expect too much when it comes to financial matters in the first month of the year. You can just try a little bit of luck on the lottery or gambling. You should watch your belongings carefully – especially be on the look-out for pickpockets when taking public transport.

Try to avoid quarrelling with your lover or spouse. You should be more flexible to appease your loved one.

Rabbit Month (18th March – 15th April)

Providence is always on the side of the big battalion

You will be quite successful this month if you have the guts to take the chances in front of you. Hesitation will make you miss a very good opportunity. Keep in mind that 'providence is always on the side of the big battalion'. You should be courageous enough to fight for your rights, but humble enough not to provoke your superiors. Mind the quality control of your products, or you will lose several clients in the near future.

The Pig's finances will be quite favourable this month. You will have additional income in the middle of the month. You will see a pretty good return on your short-term investments.

Your health is not so good this month. You should watch out for respiratory diseases. Better to put on extra layers of clothing to prevent a bad cold or influenza.

Dragon Month (16th April – 14th May)

A bad workman blames his tools

The Pig will face a series of problems in their daily work this month. You should try to handle these carefully with your own knowledge and skills. Don't find different excuses for yourself, because that won't do any good to the situation. This kind of behaviour is just like the bad workman who blames his tools without thinking how to improve his skills. Try to accept criticism from your associates. This will help you to find a way out of your difficulties.

Finances will be very poor this month. You should be conservative about financial matters, especially in purchasing expensive goods and properties. You should blame yourself and not others if you lose money in investments this month.

The Pig tends to become a severe critic this month. As a result there will be a lot of conflicts between you and your friends. You should try to cut down on this bad tendency if you want to keep your friendships.

Snake Month (15th May – 13th June)

One bad apple spoils the whole barrel

The Pig will face just as miserable a time this month as last. Pay special attention to business. Make sure that there will be no serious mistakes taking place. If you find that there is something wrong and the repair work will be beyond your ability, you should give up that project as soon as possible. Cut off its bad influence, just as you would remove a rotten apple from the barrel so it doesn't contaminate the others.

The Pig's finances will be at their lowest ebb. Cut down on those projects that lose money continuously, in order to save money for future profitable developments.

Horse Month (14th June – 12th July)

The new broom sweeps clean

The obstacles that have faced the Pig recently will be swept away this month. Make use of this chance to develop your business. There will be a new partner or a new joint venture this month, bringing fresh stimulation. If you can apply a new strategy and new methods to your business, you will have a much better chance of success in the near future. But you must watch out for those who are watching you closely, waiting for their chance to attack. Try not to give them any opportunity of doing so.

Your health is improving this month. You should go on holiday at the end of the month. This will not only give you a good chance to relax, but will also inspire your creativity in business.

The Pig will have a very good chance of meeting an attractive person for possible romance. But you should not be too ambitious, or you will spoil the whole thing in the very first instance.

Sheep Month (13th July – 10th August)

A man is known by the company he keeps

The Pig should be very careful to choose the right job and the right partner to work with this month, or you will have a lot of problems sooner or later. If you find you have chosen incorrectly, you should seriously consider changing for a new one. Otherwise, your reputation will be badly hurt. Keep an eye on your partner's financial situation – try to draw a clear line between you and do not become involved in his or her serious debts. If you choose wisely, your partner will be a boon rather than an albatross.

The Pig's finances will not be so good this month. You will be easily cheated by others. Fortunately only a very small amount of money will be involved.

Try to find out who are your real friends. A friend in need is a friend indeed. Keep away from so-called friends who do not have your best interests at heart.

Monkey Month (11th August – 9th September)

If you play with fire, you get burned

The Pig will face different kinds of problems this month. You should handle your business in the proper way and try not to use tricks or fool around. Otherwise you may find yourself embroiled in legal problems. If you play with fire, you will get burned. You must say no to any unlawful business firmly and keep away from these kinds of temptations. Apart from this, you should watch out carefully lest someone else tries to use you as 'cover' for their wrongdoings. Your firm attitude towards unlawful dealings will be paid off with the appropriate merits very soon.

Do not indulge in drugs and alcohol this month, because you will be starting off on a dead end road. Drugs and alcohol will burn you like two flames.

The Pig should not try to fool around with love, either. Again, if you play with fire, you will be badly burned sooner or later.

Rooster Month (10th September – 8th October)

It's no use crying over spilled milk

This month will be difficult, just as last month was. In fact, these two months are the most difficult times for the Pig this year. You should behave yourself and perform your duties with special care. You will meet with a series of defeats, but if you stand firm you will overcome them. Only a positive attitude can help you out of your difficulties. It is absolutely no use crying over spilled milk. Best to start all over again with a new glass.

The Pig should watch out when it comes to road safety this month. In addition, do try to relax. Your health will improve as a result.

The Pig should try not to dwell on memories of a former lover. Let bygones be bygones.

Dog Month (9th October – 7th November)

It's a poor heart that never rejoices

The Pig will walk out from the bottom of the deep valley this month. Things are looking up at the beginning of the month. You should prepare yourself for future development in the months to come. You should forget about the unhappy experiences of the past few months. Otherwise, they will become an obstruction to your future development. You should try to build up your confidence as soon as possible.

Finances will be quite steady this month. Although you won't make a lot of money, neither will you have to worry about economic problems at all.

Forgiveness is the main theme for the Pig this month. You should try to be more understanding and try your best to forgive your lover or friends for their wrongdoings. You will win in the form of harmonious relationships for a long time to come.

Pig Month (8th November – 7th December)

Moderation in all things

The Pig should try not to be too radical this month, otherwise you will bring about total defeat. The best solution is to be moderate in all things. You should try your best to avoid quarrels and disputes. A neutral standpoint will help you to survive this troublesome period of time. And, in addition, you will win others' support, because they will appreciate your neutrality.

Although the Pig's finances will be improved quite a bit, you should continue to be conservative about expenses. You will have a little luck in investments and gambling, but you should try not to be too ambitious.

You will have strong emotions regarding affairs of the heart this month. However, you should try to maintain modesty, to avoid making a serious mistake.

Mouse Month (8th December 1999 – 6th January 2000)

Good wine needs no bush

Your contributions in the past will be generally appreciated, and you will win the merits that you deserve. However, you should not remind others of these contributions over and over again, because this will have a bad effect. Your good image will be spoiled by doing so. Remember that 'good wine needs no bush'. A humble attitude will win you all. However, prepare yourself for the thunderstorm that will appear suddenly at the end of the year.

Your health will be in tip-top condition. You will be full of energy and the confidence to face any challenge. But you should keep away from alcohol.

The Pig will become the focus of attention in social gatherings. However, mind your speech and behaviour. Don't indulge in gossip or rumours about others.

Ox Month (7th January – 4th February 2000)

What cannot be cured must be endured

The Pig will face strong challenges and oppositions this month. You should try your best to face them. If these sudden problems are beyond your abilities, then you have to accept defeat with as much grace as you can. Don't be too frustrated by this. Painful experiences help us to mature. Try to find new projects to develop over the coming year.

Finances will be poor this month. You should keep a careful eye on your belongings. Make sure that the windows and doors of your house are locked safely to keep the burglars at bay.

Try to start a new friendship or a new love affair. The sorrow of losing your former love should be forgotten as soon as possible. Remember that 'what cannot be cured must be endured'.

Day-by-day Analysis of Luck

Do the right thing at the right time everyday

The charts which appear on pages 110–193 relate particularly to the art of perfect timing. The principle of daily forecasting or Chinese 'date-choosing' stems from the belief that there is a time and place for everything. The ancient Chinese believed that certain things were particularly suited to certain days. The calculation and application of this become the framework of 'date-choosing'.

Through their observations, the ancient Chinese realized that different kinds of plants needed different climates to grow, and that they had to follow nature's rules if they were to have a good harvest. For them, it therefore followed that a single day cannot be suitable for all tasks and activities. Thus, people have to choose a suitable day to do their jobs if they want to achieve good results.

The calculation involved in date-choosing can seem complicated, but fortunately there are some traditional Feng Shui rules that make things easier. The calculation is based mainly on the distribution of the different Stars on different days. Because this distribution changes from day to day, the suitable activities also change accordingly.

Format

The format of these forecast charts (which run from 1st January to 31st December, 1999) is as follows:

The first two columns list the month and day.

The third column lists the Favourable Activities for that day.

Days highlighted in **boldface** type indicate a very fortunate day, those in normal type indicate a fair-to-middling day, and those in *italics* indicate an unlucky day.

Try not to schedule important activities for unlucky days; however, if you cannot avoid doing a certain job on an unlucky day, choose the lucky hours of that day (column four). This alternative is sometimes quite effective.

Not all hours are suitable even on a fortunate day. Choosing lucky hours can add to the effect of a fortuitous day, while less lucky hours can undermine this effect.

The ancient Chinese believed that there were good directions and bad directions, and that these changed on a daily basis. The three most important were the Direction of Happiness (column five), Direction of Opportunity (column six) and the Direction of Wealth (column seven).

The Direction of Happiness is an auspicious pointer for seating at weddings, birthday parties, etc., to ensure happiness for all participants.

If looking for good investments and a good income, sitting in the Direction of Wealth for a given day will enhance your efforts.

If looking for promotion or a breakthrough in your career or in your studies, sitting in the Direction of Opportunity for a given day will foster success.

Explanations

The 32 activities listed are divided into seven categories:

A Spiritual Rites
B Social Interactions
C Out and About
D Commercial Activities
E Cleaning
F Household Activities
G Outdoor Pursuits

Spiritual Rites
(1) Worship

The ancient Chinese used to worship different kinds of gods and spirits. For instance, they would worship the gods of Heaven, the gods of Nature, and the honourable dead such as historical figures and their own ancestors. In order to purify themselves before the gods or honourable dead, they would not eat any meat nor take any wine for a period of time, and would take a bath shortly before the worship ceremony. According to Chinese tradition, there were certain days especially suitable for worship.

(2) Blessing

The ancient Chinese would go to the temples and ask the monks there to perform the blessing ceremony for them when they were experiencing troubles over a period of time. They hoped that their luck would change from bad to good as a result. In order to have a better result, they would choose a suitable day for blessing.

There is a big difference between 'Blessing' and 'Worship'. The former refers to the blessing of living people, while the latter refers to the memorial ceremony for the gods or the honourable dead.

(3) Burial

The ancient Chinese believed that whether the newly dead were buried properly or not would have strong influences over the fate of their descendants. As a result, they would sincerely ask the Feng Shui masters to choose a good place and good time to bury their newly dead family member. They considered that the burial timing must be right, or the Feng Shui of the grave would be minimized no matter how good it was.

According to the Chinese tradition, there were some days especially suitable for burial of the dead. Not only the living descendants would be benefited, but also the buried dead could rest peacefully in the grave as a result.

Social Interactions

(4) Engagement

The procedures of an ancient Chinese marriage were very complicated and tediously long. From engagement to wedding, it would take months or even years. The parents of the young couples insisted that both engagement and wedding should take place on lucky days to ensure a happy ending and a fruitful marriage with many offspring. During the engagement, the parents of both families had to exchange gifts as commitments to each other.

(5) Wedding

The meaning of marriage in ancient China was quite different from that of nowadays. The ancient Chinese marriage was considered to be the tool of reproduction so that the family could keep on growing from generation to generation. The emphasis of an ancient marriage was on reproduction rather than on true love between the young couple.

The parents would therefore choose a lucky day for the wedding ceremony of their youngsters, to ensure as many descendants as possible. Date-choosing for weddings has been a primary concern in Chinese society for centuries.

(6) Social Gathering

Friendship and harmonious relationship were highly appreciated in ancient China. People would choose a lucky day to meet their new and old friends. They would clean themselves and prepare gifts before the meeting to show their sincerity. They believed that there would be a happy gathering, mutual understanding and agreement as a result.

This can apply to formal and informal social gatherings of different natures, such as birthday parties, fund-raising events, exhibitions and conferences in modern society.

(7) Start Learning

The ancient Chinese would study very hard to pass the Civil Examination, because they could change their social status from the common class to the ruling class if they performed well. The parents would urge their youngsters to go to school at an early age. The 'Start learning' ceremony was one of the most important events in a man's life, because not too many people would have the chance of receiving an education. The ceremony was very serious and would be performed only on the lucky day, to ensure success in the future examination.

Nowadays this can also apply to the starting of different kinds of lessons, such as driving, dancing, singing and so on.

Out and About
(8) Moving

The ancient Chinese were very reluctant to move, either to a new home or a new town, because they were afraid to give up the old and start all over again in a new place. In order to increase their confidence, they would choose a lucky day for moving. They believed that this would make their new lives easier and smoother.

(9) Travelling

The ancient Chinese used to bind themselves to their cultivated lands because all their wealth, property and relatives were closely connected with their lands. As a result, they were very reluctant to travel. Besides which, traffic systems were not well developed at that time, so that travelling would be quite uncomfortable and dangerous. If they had to travel, they would choose a lucky day to start their journey. They hoped that a good beginning would bring about a good ending.

Commercial Activities

(10) Grand Opening

The ancient Chinese merchants would choose a very lucky day for the grand opening of their shops in order to have a good beginning to their business. Usually, lion dance and fire-crackers would be used during the ceremony to bring good luck to the shop.

Nowadays, the moment of ribbon-cutting and champagne toasting should take place at the lucky hour of the lucky day, to ensure a successful venture.

(11) Signing Contracts

Even in ancient China it was the norm for contracts to be drawn up and signed to confirm any business or legal transactions. In order to avoid arguments and conflicts in the future, the parties involved would choose a lucky day to sign these contracts.

This can apply to the signing of different kinds of commercial and legal documents in the modern world.

(12) Trading

Commercial activities were not common in ancient China, nor were merchants well appreciated. However, different kinds of trading would take place in different ways, such as trading of crops, domestic animals, fields and houses. Both the buyer and the seller would choose a lucky day for trading in order to bring about the greatest possible mutual benefit.

This can apply to the trading of different kinds of business in the modern world. People can earn more profit if they pick a lucky day for their trading, according to traditional Chinese beliefs.

(13) Money Collecting

The ancient Chinese considered that money in the market was similar to fish in the river: neither was easy to catch. Just as the fishermen would wait for the right tide to catch fish, the Chinese would choose the right timing to collect money. If they chose the wrong time to do so, then they would not only have difficulties in collecting the money, but also would have difficulties keeping hold of it.

Cleaning

(14) House Cleaning

The ancient Chinese considered that the house of a family was equivalent to the body of a person. Both should be kept clean at all times, or disease and bad luck would ensue.

People would go to the doctor to clear up accumulated poisonous deposits inside the body when they were sick. In much the same way, people would choose a lucky day to clean up their homes thoroughly when they'd been experiencing bad luck over a period of time. They hoped that their bad luck would be swept away with the dirt from their homes.

(15) Bathing

The meaning of 'bath' in Chinese date-choosing is quite different from that of the daily bath in the modern world. In ancient times, the Chinese would clean themselves thoroughly before important ceremonies to show their purity and sincerity. They would carefully choose a suitable day to take this ritual bath. In addition, some would keep to a vegetarian diet for a period of time in order to purify their bodies completely inside and out.

If they had been experiencing bad luck for a period of time, they would add some kind of herbs to the bath water to wash away the bad luck.

(16) Hair Cutting

The ancient Chinese had a very strong feeling about their hair because it was regarded as a symbol of their ego. Without a proper hair style, it was felt they would lose all sense of self and self-esteem. History tells us that thousands and thousands of Chinese were killed by the new ruler between 1644 and 1645 simply because they refused to cut their hair.

The ancient Chinese believed that to cut hair on lucky days would bring good luck.

(17) Tailoring

The ancient Chinese of the common class had few clothes because they couldn't afford them. They would have clothes made for them only for very special occasions, such as weddings, birthdays and New Year's Day. They would choose a lucky day to have fittings at the tailor because they believed this would bring good luck to them.

Household Activities

(18) Bed Set-up

The main entrance, stove and sleeping area are considered the three essential factors in Feng Shui studies. Therefore, to set up a bed in the proper place at the proper time in a new house is a prime concern of the Feng Shui master. If it is properly done, the person who sleeps in the bed will enjoy good sleep and, consequently, good health.

If people wanted to get a new bed but a Feng Shui master was not available to help them, they would choose a lucky day from the calendar to do so.

(19) Stove Set-up

The stove is considered important because it is closely related with the health of the whole family. According to Feng Shui theory, if

the stove is set up in the wrong part of the kitchen, the food prepared from there will spoil the health of the family members.

(20) Door-fixing

The ancient Chinese used to pay special attention to the main
entrance of their homes because of security and Feng Shui reasons. They considered that a pair of sturdy doors at the main
entrance, acting as the main gate to guard them from being
attacked by robbers and gangsters, were of primary importance.
They also considered that if the door at the main entrance opened
in the right direction to let the good *Chi* (positive energy) flow
into the house, then the Feng Shui of that house would be greatly
upgraded. No matter the reason, they would choose a lucky day to
fix the door to their main entrance.

(21) Crack Refilling

The ancient Chinese considered that the small cracks and large
holes that appear in walls and anywhere else in the home or workplace should be filled in as soon as possible. This stemmed in part
from practical reasons: if there were no holes, then no rats, snakes
or poisonous insects or animals could live there. The work usually
involves using cement and different herbs to fill up the cracks and
holes. They would choose a suitable day to do this kind of work,
but not necessarily a very lucky day.

(22) Decorating

The ancient Chinese considered the wall of a house as important
as the face of a human being. If there were some cracks or dirt on
the wall, that meant the owner lost 'face'. They would hire workers
to repair and redecorate in a suitable fashion. They believed that
their luck would be changed after that.

This can apply to decorating with paint or wall paper. It is also
applicable to the practice of tearing down old walls and building
new ones.

(23) Construction

The ancient Chinese would break the ground of the site at the beginning of each construction. In order to please the guardian spirits of the earth, they would kill a rooster and pig as sacrifices to them as part of the ground-breaking ceremony. The ceremony had to take place at the lucky hour of the lucky day to ensure the safety of the construction. They deeply believed that to break the ground at the wrong time would lead to many problems and accidents during construction.

(24) Ditch-digging

The ancient Chinese villagers used to dig ditches in and out of their cultivated lands and houses for irrigation and washing. They would carefully choose the right direction to dig the ditches at the right time in order to let the good *Chi* flow in together with the water. According to the Feng Shui theory, the water should flow in from the good direction and flow out towards the bad direction.

This can apply to any piping work in the modern house. The building of a swimming pool is another example.

(25) Passage-fixing

The passages of a house were considered to be as important as the blood vessels of a human body. Therefore, good maintenance of the passages were necessary in order to keep good Feng Shui. If there was any damage, then it would be fitting to repair it as soon as possible. The ancient Chinese believed that to change a rough passage into a smooth one would change their luck from bad to good. People would choose a lucky day for fixing passages in and out of their homes.

(26) Nursery Set-up

To have more offspring in order to increase the family was the prime concern of the ancient Chinese. Therefore, they would be very serious about choosing a lucky day to set up a nursery room for their baby. They believed that a good nursery would bring a healthy baby with good fortune.

This can also be applied to the set-up of a cot or Moses basket for a newborn baby.

Outdoor Pursuits
(27) Hunting

Hunting was not so common in ancient China because it was the privilege of the noble class. But gradually, the common people would go hunting on a much smaller scale on some special occasions. In order to ensure a safe and productive hunt, they would choose a lucky day to go hunting.

(28) Capturing

According to Chinese tradition, there was a difference between hunting and catching. Hunting involved killing with weapons, while catching referred to catching animals and birds alive with nets or traps. The former was the privilege of the noble class, while the latter was a common practice among the lower classes.

According to the traditional Chinese calendar, there were some days especially good for catching.

(29) Planting

The ancient Chinese paid special attention to planting because agriculture was their major source of income. Besides the planting of major crops, they would have some other crops to supplement their income. They believed that the harvest of any crop would be determined by the day on which that was planted. If they didn't choose the right time to start with, then their harvest would be spoiled.

This can also apply to the planting of flowers and fruit trees on a smaller scale in private gardens. The plants will grow much better if a suitable day for planting is chosen according to the classic Chinese calendar.

(30) Animal Acquiring

The ancient Chinese farmers would raise some animals and fowl such as pigs, sheep, ducks and chickens to supplement their income. Because infections were very common among these kinds of domestic creatures at that time, so the farmers had to be very cautious about raising them. When they wanted to bring in some new animals, they would choose a lucky day to do so. They believed that an unlucky day would bring in bad luck together with the animals, especially in the form of infections and disease.

This can apply to the buying of small domestic pets, such as cats, rabbits, dogs, canaries, parrots, etc. To buy these pets or to accept them as gifts on a lucky day is believed to ensure their healthy growth and also a close relationship between the animals and their owners.

(31) Fishing

Chinese fishermen used to go out to the open sea for fishing with sampans or junks. These small wooden boats were not strong enough for the rough and dangerous seas. Any accidents could happen suddenly. They might end up losing their boats or even their lives.

In order to avoid these kinds of tragedies, the fishermen would set up strict rules to be followed among themselves; choosing a lucky day for fishing was one of them. They believed that this would bring them back safely with an abundance of fish.

This also applies to angling in any form.

(32) Net Weaving

Fishermen used nets to catch fish in the water, while catchers used nets to traps animals in the forest. Therefore, nets were very important in ancient Chinese villages. Both the fishermen and the catchers would take good care of their nets. They would choose a lucky day to prepare new nets or to repair old ones.

This can apply to the preparation of objects that are similar to nets, such as fences, drapes and curtains.

Date	Day	Favourable Activities
Jan 1	**Fri**	Grand Opening, Trading, Moving, Hair Cutting Wedding, Construction, Travelling
2	**Sat**	Grand Opening, Travelling, Net Weaving Signing Contracts, Trading, Construction Money Collecting, Planting
3	Sun	Construction, Decorating
4	**Mon**	Wedding, Net Weaving, Tailoring, Door-fixing Construction, Engagement, Trading
5	Tue	Worship, Capturing
6	Wed	Travelling, Hair Cutting, Capturing
7	Thu	Unlucky Day Not Suitable for Important Activities
8	Fri	Unlucky Day Not Suitable for Important Activities
9	**Sat**	Construction, Engagement, Wedding, Travelling Moving, Grand Opening, Start Learning, Burial
10	Sun	Worship, Hunting

Lucky Hours			Direction of Happiness	Direction of Opportunity	Direction of Wealth
23-01	01-03	07-09	SE	E	S
09-11	17-19	19-21			
03-05	07-09	11-13	NE	NE	SE
17-19	19-21				
03-05	05-07	13-15	NW	SW	SE
19-21	21-23				
09-11	17-19	21-23	SW	W	W
01-03	09-11	13-15	S	W	W
17-19	19-21				
05-07	09-11	17-19	SE	SW	N
03-05	05-07	09-11	NW	SW	NE
11-13					
01-03	07-09	09-11	NW	SW	E
11-13					
03-05	07-09	09-11	SW	NE	E
11-13					
03-05	05-07	09-11	S	E	S
19-21	21-23				

Date	Day	Favourable Activities
Jan 11	Mon	Worship, Door-fixing, Stove Set-up
12	Tue	Net Weaving, Tailoring, Bathing, Burial
13	**Wed**	Worship, Blessing, Engagement, Tailoring Animal Acquiring
14	**Thu**	Moving, Bathing, House Cleaning, Door-fixing Engagement
15	Fri	Worship, Door-fixing, Stove Set-up Decorating
16	Sat	Decorating
17	**Sun**	Signing Contracts, Trading, Engagement Construction, Stove Set-up
18	**Mon**	Blessing, Wedding, Planting, Travelling Engagement, Construction, Moving, Burial
19	*Tue*	Unlucky Day Not Suitable for Important Activities
20	*Wed*	Unlucky Day Not Suitable for Important Activities

Lucky Hours			Direction of Happiness	Direction of Opportunity	Direction of Wealth
03-05	05-07	07-09	SE	E	S
11-13	19-21	21-23			
23-01	01-03	03-05	NE	NE	SE
07-09					
23-01	01-03	03-05	NW	N	SE
05-07	17-19				
23-01	05-07	11-13	SW	W	W
17-19					
03-05	11-13		S	NW	W
01-03	05-07	09-11	SE	NE	N
17-19					
23-01	03-05	11-13	NE	SW	N
01-03	03-05	11-13	NW	SW	E
17-19					
03-05	05-07	09-11	SW	S	E
11-13					
23-01	01-03	05-07	S	E	S
07-09	09-11	17-19			

Date	Day	Favourable Activities
Jan 21	**Thu**	Start Learning, Grand Opening, Engagement Wedding, Trading, Moving, Burial, Travelling
22	Fri	Worship, Capturing
23	**Sat**	Blessing, Construction, Grand Opening Start Learning, Social Gathering, Tailoring Nursery Set-up
24	Sun	Net Weaving, Bathing, Burial
25	Mon	Worship, Signing Contracts
26	**Tue**	Engagement, Moving, Stove Set-up, Bathing House Cleaning, Bed Set-up
27	**Wed**	Blessing, Grand Opening, Start Learning, Net Weaving, Engagement, Money Collecting
28	Thu	Worship, Decorating
29	**Fri**	Blessing, Construction, Signing Contracts Trading, Moving, Animal Acquiring
30	**Sat**	Hair Cutting, Bathing, Capturing, Hunting Bed Set-up
31	Sun	Unlucky Day Not Suitable for Important Activities

Lucky Hours			Direction of Happiness	Direction of Opportunity	Direction of Wealth
23-01 01-03 03-05 07-09 09-11			SE	SE	S
01-03 03-05 05-07 09-11			NE	NE	SE
23-01 01-03 03-05 05-07			NW	SW	SE
23-01 01-03 09-11 17-19 19-21 21-23			SW	W	W
23-01 09-11 11-13 17-19 21-23			S	NW	W
01-03 05-07 07-09 09-11 11-13			SE	NE	N
23-01 03-05 05-07 11-13			NE	SW	N
01-03 03-05 07-09 09-11 11-13 21-23			NW	NE	E
01-03 03-05 09-11 11-13 19-21			SW	NE	E
01-03 03-05 05-07 09-11 21-23			S	E	S
23-01 03-05 05-07 09-11 11-13 19-21			SE	E	S

Date	Day	Favourable Activities
Feb 1	Mon	Unlucky Day Not Suitable for Important Activities
2	**Tue**	Wedding, Travelling, Grand Opening, Trading Construction, Start Learning, Burial
3	Wed	Unlucky Day Not Suitable for Important Activities
4	Thu	Worship, House Cleaning, Start Learning Bathing
5	Fri	Worship, Hair Cutting, House Cleaning Bathing
6	Sat	Decorating, Crack Refilling
7	Sun	Signing Contracts, Trading, Money Collecting Animal Acquiring
8	**Mon**	Blessing, Construction, Wedding, Travelling Trading, Signing Contracts, Moving, Burial
9	**Tue**	Grand Opening, Moving, Blessing, Trading Wedding, Travelling, Construction, Burial
10	Wed	Unlucky Day Not Suitable for Important Activities

Lucky Hours			Direction of Happiness	Direction of Opportunity	Direction of Wealth
23-01	01-03	07-09	NE	SW	SE
09-11	15-17	17-19			
23-01	01-03	03-05	NW	SW	SE
07-09	15-17	17-19			
23-01	03-05	05-07	SW	W	W
09-11	15-17	17-19			
19-21	21-23				
01-03	03-05	11-13	S	W	W
19-21	21-23				
01-03	05-07	07-09	SE	NE	N
09-11					
23-01	03-05	05-0-7	NE	N	N
09-11					
01-03	03-05	05-07	NW	NE	E
07-09					
03-05	05-07	09-11	SW	NE	E
11-13	19-21				
01-03	03-05	05-07	S	E	S
09-11	21-23				
23-01	05-07	07-09	SE	SE	S
09-11	19-21				

Date	Day	Favourable Activities
Feb 11	**Thu**	Engagement, Construction, Trading, Wedding Animal Acquiring, Grand Opening, Travelling
12	Fri	Net Weaving, Fishing, Capturing, Blessing
13	Sat	Unlucky Day Not Suitable for Important Activities
14	Sun	Unlucky Day Not Suitable for Important Activities
15	Mon	Start Learning, Decorating
16	Tue	Chinese New Year (Solar Eclipse) Not Suitable for Important Activities
17	Wed	Worship, Bathing, Start Learning, Bed Set-up
18	Thu	Worship, Net Weaving, Decorating Crack Refilling
19	**Fri**	Signing Contracts, Social Gathering, Trading Bed Set-up, Engagement, Burial
20	**Sat**	Grand Opening, Engagement, Hair Cutting Travelling, House Cleaning, Trading

Lucky Hours			Direction of Happiness	Direction of Opportunity	Direction of Wealth
01-03	03-05	13-15	NE	SW	SE
23-01	03-05	05-07	NW	SW	SE
19-21	21-23				
23-01	01-03	09-11	SW	W	W
13-15	19-21	21-23			
01-03	11-13	13-15	S	NW	W
21-23					
01-03	05-07	11-13	SE	NE	N
13-15					
23-01	03-05	05-07	NE	SW	N
11-13	13-15				
01-03	13-15		NW	NE	E
01-03	03-05	05-07	SW	NE	E
09-11	11-13	21-23			
01-03	03-05	05-07	S	E	S
13-15	19-21				
23-01	03-05	05-07	SE	E	S
19-21					

Date	Day	Favourable Activities
Feb 21	Sun	Blessing, Social Gathering, Net Weaving Tailoring
22	Mon	Passage-fixing
23	**Tue**	Grand Opening, Travelling, Capturing, Planting Construction, Social Gathering, Moving, Burial
24	**Wed**	Grand Opening, Travelling, Capturing, Planting Construction, Social Gathering, Moving, Burial
25	Thu	Unlucky Day Not Suitable for Important Activities
26	Fri	Unlucky Day Not Suitable for Important Activities
27	Sat	Start Learning
28	**Sun**	Construction, Tailoring, Travelling, Moving Grand Opening, Animal Acquiring

Lucky Hours	Direction of Happiness	Direction of Opportunity	Direction of Wealth
23-01 01-03 03-05 07-09 21-23	NE	SW	SE
23-01 01-03 19-21	NW	N	SE
09-11 11-13 19-21 21-23	SW	NW	W
09-11 11-13 13-15 21-23	S	NW	W
01-03 07-09 09-11 13-15	SE	SW	N
23-01 07-09 09-11 11-13 13-15	NE	SW	N
01-03 11-13 13-15	NW	SW	E
01-03 03-05 05-07 11-13 13-15 19-21	SW	S	E

Date	Day	Favourable Activities
Mar 1	**Mon**	Worship, Engagement, Grand Opening, Moving Construction, Travelling, Wedding, Blessing
2	Tue	Bed Set-up, Stove Set-up
3	Wed	Signing Contracts, Trading, Social Gathering Animal Acquiring
4	**Thu**	Wedding, House Cleaning, Trading, Travelling Construction, Signing Contracts, Burial
5	**Fri**	Travelling, Engagement, Wedding, Construction Worship, Blessing, Grand Opening, Moving
6	**Sat**	Grand Opening, Engagement, Money Collecting Trading, Signing Contracts, Blessing
7	Sun	Worship, Passage-fixing, Tailoring Decorating
8	**Mon**	Construction, Grand Opening, Signing Contracts Bed Set-up, Moving, Money Collecting, Travelling, Burial
9	Tue	Bathing, House Cleaning, Capturing, Fishing
10	Wed	Unlucky Day Not Suitable for Important Activities

Lucky Hours			Direction of Happiness	Direction of Opportunity	Direction of Wealth
23-01 01-03 03-05 05-07 07-09 09-11 13-15			S	E	S
23-01 01-03 07-09 09-11 19-21			SE	E	S
03-05 07-09 13-15 19-21			NE	NE	SE
03-05 05-07 13-15 19-21 21-23			NW	SW	SE
09-11 21-23			SW	W	W
01-03 09-11 11-13 13-15 19-21			S	W	W
05-07 09-11 13-15 15-17			SE	SW	N
03-05 05-07 09-11 11-13 13-15 15-17			NE	SW	N
01-03 07-09 09-11 11-13 13-15 15-17			NW	SW	E
03-05 07-09 09-11 11-13			SW	NE	E

Date	Day	Favourable Activities
Mar 11	Thu	Trading, Signing Contracts, Fishing, Stove Set-up
12	Fri	Stove Set-up, Tailoring, Bathing
13	Sat	Worship, Bathing, Hair Cutting, Capturing
14	**Sun**	Wedding, Engagement, Nursery Set-up Start Learning, Moving, Ditch digging, Travelling Construction
15	**Mon**	Decorating, Net Weaving, Signing Contracts Trading, Tailoring, Planting
16	**Tue**	Travelling, Blessing, Moving, Trading Engagement, Signing Contracts
17	Wed	House Cleaning, Bathing, Hair Cutting Travelling
18	Thu	Engagement, Tailoring, Animal Acquiring
19	Fri	Worship, Passage-fixing, Decorating
20	Sat	Unlucky Day Not Suitable for Important Activities

Lucky Hours			Direction of Happiness	Direction of Opportunity	Direction of Wealth
03-05	05-07	09-11	S	E	S
13-15	19-21	21-23			
03-05	05-07	07-09	SE	E	S
11-13	19-21	21-23			
23-01	01-03	03-05	NE	NE	SE
07-09	13-15	15-17			
23-01	01-03	03-05	NW	N	SE
05-07	15-17				
23-01	05-07	11-13	SW	W	W
03-05	11-13	13-15	S	NW	W
01-03	05-07	09-11	SE	NE	N
13-15	15-17				
23-01	03-05	11-13	NE	SW	N
13-15	15-17				
01-03	03-05	11-13	NW	SW	E
13-15	15-17				
03-05	05-07	09-11	SW	S	E
11-13	15-17				

Date	Day	Favourable Activities
Mar 21	Sun	Hunting, House Cleaning, Bathing
22	Mon	Unlucky Day Not Suitable for Important Activities
23	**Tue**	Travelling, Moving, Wedding, Bed Set-up Trading, Grand Opening, Construction, Burial
24	**Wed**	Start Learning, Net Weaving, Animal Acquiring Moving, Construction, Travelling, Tailoring
25	Thu	Net Weaving, Capturing
26	**Fri**	Wedding, Ditch-digging, Construction Engagement, Animal Acquiring, Moving, Travelling
27	**Sat**	Signing Contracts, Trading, Net Weaving Decorating, Tailoring
28	Sun	Worship, Social Gathering
29	Mon	House Cleaning, Bathing, Hair Cutting Travelling
30	**Tue**	Worship, Grand Opening, Money Collecting Social Gathering, Net Weaving, Trading
31	Wed	Worship, Passage-fixing, Decorating

Lucky Hours			Direction of Happiness	Direction of Opportunity	Direction of Wealth
23-01	01-03	05-07	S	E	S
07-09	09-11	13-15			
23-01	01-03	03-05	SE	SE	S
07-09	09-11	15-17			
01-03	03-05	05-07	NE	NE	SE
09-11	13-15				
23-01	01-03	03-05	NW	SW	SE
05-07	13-15				
23-01	01-03	09-11	SW	W	W
19-21	21-23				
23-01	09-11	11-13	S	NW	W
21-23					
01-03	05-07	07-09	SE	NE	N
09-11	11-13	13-15			
23-01	03-05	05-07	NE	SW	N
11-13	13-15				
01-03	03-05	07-09	NW	NE	E
09-11	11-13	13-15			
21-23					
01-03	03-05	09-11	SW	NE	E
11-13	13-15	19-21			
01-03	03-05	05-07	S	E	S
09-11	13-15	21-23			

Date	Day	Favourable Activities
Apr 1	**Thu**	Engagement, Wedding, Travelling, Trading Construction, Moving, Grand Opening, Burial
2	Fri	Worship, House Cleaning, Bathing, Capturing
3	*Sat*	Unlucky Day Not Suitable for Important Activities
4	**Sun**	Worship, Fishing, Capturing, Hunting Tailoring
5	**Mon**	Blessing, Social Gathering, Bed Set-up, Planting Travelling, Start Learning, Moving, Engagement
6	**Tue**	Start Learning, Signing Contracts, Door-fixing Grand Opening, Wedding, Moving, Travelling Trading
7	Wed	Worship, Money Collecting, Animal Acquiring Capturing
8	**Thu**	Grand Opening, Nursery Set-up, Signing Contracts Travelling, Moving, Trading, Construction
9	Fri	Worship, Decorating, Crack Refilling
10	Sat	Worship, House Cleaning, Tailoring

Lucky Hours			Direction of Happiness	Direction of Opportunity	Direction of Wealth
23-01	03-05	05-07	SE	E	S
09-11	11-13	19-21			
23-01	01-03	07-09	NE	SW	SE
09-11	13-15	15-17			
23-01	01-03	03-05	NW	SW	SE
07-09	15-17				
23-01	03-05	05-07	SW	W	W
09-11	15-17	19-21			
21-23					
01-03	03-05	11-13	S	W	W
13-15	21-23				
01-03	05-07	07-09	SE	NE	N
09-11	15-17				
23-01	03-05	05-07	NE	N	N
09-11	15-17				
01-03	03-05	05-07	NW	NE	E
07-09					
03-05	05-07	09-11	SW	NE	E
11-13					
01-03	03-05	05-07	S	E	S
09-11	21-23				

Date	Day	Favourable Activities
Apr 11	Sun	Unlucky Day Not Suitable for Important Activities
12	Mon	Worship, Net Weaving
13	Tue	Hunting, Fishing, Net Weaving, Decorating
14	Wed	Worship, Bathing, House Cleaning, Door-fixing
15	Thu	Unlucky Day Not Suitable for Important Activities
16	Fri	Unlucky Day Not Suitable for Important Activities
17	Sat	Planting, Fishing, Bathing, House Cleaning
18	**Sun**	Signing Contracts, Grand Opening, Construction Start Learning, Trading, Travelling, Wedding
19	Mon	Worship, Animal Acquiring, Capturing, Fishing
20	**Tue**	Travelling, Moving, Start Learning, Trading Construction, Grand Opening, Wedding

Lucky Hours			Direction of Happiness	Direction of Opportunity	Direction of Wealth
23-01 05-07 07-09 09-11 15-17			SE	SE	S
01-03 03-05 13-15			NE	SW	SE
23-01 03-05 05-07 15-17 21-23			NW	SW	SE
23-01 01-03 09-11 13-15 15-17 21-23			SW	W	W
01-03 11-13 13-15 21-23			S	NW	W
01-03 05-07 11-13 13-15 15-17			SE	NE	N
23-01 03-05 05-07 11-13 13-15 15-17			NE	SW	N
01-03 13-15 15-17			NW	NE	E
01-03 03-05 05-07 09-11 11-13 15-17 21-23			SW	NE	E
01-03 03-05 05-07 13-15			S	E	S

Date	Day	Favourable Activities
Apr 21	Wed	Decorating, Crack Refilling
22	Thu	Worship
23	Fri	House Cleaning, Stove Set-up, Hair Cutting Bathing
24	Sat	Worship
25	Sun	Passage-fixing, Decorating
26	Mon	Bathing, House Cleaning, Door-fixing Animal Acquiring
27	Tue	Unlucky Day Not Suitable for Important Activities
28	Wed	Unlucky Day Not Suitable for Important Activities
29	**Thu**	Social Gathering, Bathing, Bed Set-up, Fishing Planting, Animal Acquiring
30	**Fri**	Grand Opening, Signing Contracts, Travelling Wedding, Engagement, Trading, Construction Burial

Lucky Hours	Direction of Happiness	Direction of Opportunity	Direction of Wealth
23-01 03-05 05-07	SE	E	S
23-01 01-03 03-05 07-09 13-15 21-23	NE	SW	SE
23-01 01-03 15-17	NW	N	SE
09-11 11-13 15-17 21-23	SW	NW	W
09-11 11-13 15-17 21-23	S	NW	W
01-03 07-09 09-11 13-15 15-17	SE	SW	N
23-01 07-09 09-11 11-13 13-15 15-17	NE	SW	N
01-03 11-13 13-15 15-17	NW	SW	E
01-03 03-05 05-07 11-13 13-15	SW	S	E
23-01 01-03 03-05 05-07 07-09 09-11 13-15	S	E	S

Date	Day	Favourable Activities
May 1	Sat	Worship, Capturing, Hunting, Animal Acquiring
2	**Sun**	Grand Opening, Signing Contracts, Construction Trading, Ditch-digging, Travelling, Planting, Moving
3	Mon	Decorating, Crack Refilling
4	Tue	Worship
5	*Wed*	Unlucky Day Not Suitable for Important Activities
6	**Thu**	Worship, House Cleaning, Stove Set-up Door-fixing, Bathing, Burial
7	Fri	Worship, Net Weaving, Crack Refilling Nursery Set-up
8	**Sat**	Grand Opening, Signing Contracts, Travelling Moving, Trading, Construction, Burial
9	*Sun*	Unlucky Day Not Suitable for Important Activities
10	Mon	Hair Cutting, Bathing, Net Weaving, Capturing

Lucky Hours			Direction of Happiness	Direction of Opportunity	Direction of Wealth
23-01	01-03	07-09	SE	E	S
09-11	15-17				
03-05	07-09	13-15	NE	NE	SE
03-05	05-07	13-15	NW	SW	SE
15-17	21-23				
09-11	15-17	21-23	SW	W	W
01-03	09-11	11-13	S	W	W
13-15					
05-07	09-11	13-15	SE	SW	N
15-17					
03-05	05-07	09-11	NE	SW	N
11-13	13-15	15-17			
01-03	07-09	09-11	NW	SW	E
11-13	13-15	15-17			
03-05	07-09	09-11	SW	NE	E
11-13					
03-05	05-07	09-11	S	E	S
13-15	19-21				

Date	Day	Favourable Activities
May 11	*Tue*	Unlucky Day Not Suitable for Important Activities
12	Wed	Worship, Stove Set-up, Bathing, Burial
13	**Thu**	Grand Opening, Construction, Start Learning Blessing, Wedding, Door-fixing, Burial
14	**Fri**	Wedding, Signing Contracts, Engagement Moving, Travelling, Trading
15	**Sat**	Worship, Blessing, Door-fixing, Stove Set-up Planting, Start Learning
16	Sun	Decorating, Crack Refilling
17	Mon	Net Weaving
18	**Tue**	Worship, Travelling, House Cleaning, Wedding Moving, Construction, Planting, Burial
19	Wed	Worship, Nursery Set-up
20	Thu	Worship, Passage-fixing, House Cleaning Bathing

Lucky Hours	Direction of Happiness	Direction of Opportunity	Direction of Wealth
03-05 05-07 07-09 11-13 19-21	SE	E	S
23-01 01-03 03-05 07-09 13-15 15-17	NE	NE	SE
23-01 01-03 03-05 05-07 15-17	NW	N	SE
23-01 05-07 11-13	SW	W	W
03-05 11-13 13-15	S	NW	W
01-03 05-07 09-11 13-15 15-17	SE	NE	N
23-01 03-05 11-13 13-15 15-17	NE	SW	N
01-03 03-05 11-13 13-15 15-17	NW	SW	E
03-05 05-07 09-11 11-13 15-17	SW	S	E
23-01 01-03 05-07 07-09 09-11 13-15	S	E	S

Date	Day	Favourable Activities
May 21	Fri	Unlucky Day Not Suitable for Important Activities
22	**Sat**	Wedding, Bed Set-up, Hair Cutting, Bathing Construction, Capturing
23	Sun	Unlucky Day Not Suitable for Important Activities
24	**Mon**	Construction, Planting, Bed Set-up, Tailoring Travelling, Moving
25	**Tue**	Grand Opening, Signing Contracts, Engagement Animal Acquiring, Travelling, Construction, Trading
26	Wed	Fishing, Capturing
27	Thu	Worship, Start Learning, Social Gathering Travelling
28	**Fri**	Worship, Signing Contracts, Trading, Travelling Construction, Burial
29	**Sat**	Blessing, Engagement, Wedding, Tailoring Moving, Animal Acquiring
30	**Sun**	Grand Opening, Hair Cutting, House Cleaning Construction, Travelling, Worship, Blessing Burial
31	Mon	Worship

Lucky Hours			Direction of Happiness	Direction of Opportunity	Direction of Wealth
23-01 01-03 03-05 07-09 09-11 15-17			SE	SE	S
01-03 03-05 05-07 09-11 13-15			NE	NE	SE
23-01 01-03 03-05 05-07 13-15			NW	SW	SE
23-01 01-03 09-11 19-21			SW	W	W
23-01 09-11 11-13			S	NW	W
01-03 05-07 07-09 09-11 11-13 13-15			SE	NE	N
23-01 03-05 05-07 11-13 13-15			NE	SW	N
01-03 03-05 07-09 09-11 11-13 13-15			NW	NE	E
01-03 03-05 09-11 11-13 13-15 19-21			SW	NE	E
01-03 03-05 05-07 09-11 13-15			S	E	S
23-01 03-05 05-07 09-11 11-13 19-21			SE	E	S

Date	Day	Favourable Activities
Jun 1	Tue	Worship, House Cleaning, Passage-fixing Bathing
2	*Wed*	Unlucky Day Not Suitable for Important Activities
3	Thu	Worship, Social Gathering, Hair Cutting Capturing
4	*Fri*	Unlucky Day Not Suitable for Important Activities
5	Sat	Social Gathering, Bathing, Stove Set-up Tailoring
6	Sun	Engagement, Bed Set-up, Construction, Burial
7	**Mon**	Start Learning, Grand Opening, Construction Travelling, Signing Contracts, Money Collecting Trading, Burial
8	Tue	Worship, Decorating
9	**Wed**	Blessing, Planting, Signing Contracts, Moving Start Learning, Engagement, Travelling Nursery Set-up
10	*Thu*	Unlucky Day Not Suitable for Important Activities

Lucky Hours	Direction of Happiness	Direction of Opportunity	Direction of Wealth
23-01 01-03 07-09 09-11 13-15 15-17	NE	SW	SE
23-01 01-03 03-05 07-09 15-17	NW	SW	SE
23-01 03-05 05-07 15-17 19-21	SW	W	W
01-03 03-05 11-13 13-15 19-21	S	W	W
01-03 05-07 07-09 09-11 15-17	SE	NE	N
23-01 03-05 05-07 09-11 15-17	NE	N	N
01-03 03-05 05-07 07-09	NW	NE	E
03-05 05-07 09-11 11-13	SW	NE	E
01-03 03-05 05-07 09-11 21-23	S	E	S
05-07 07-09 09-11 15-17 19-21	SE	SE	S

Date	Day	Favourable Activities
Jun 11	Fri	Worship
12	**Sat**	Wedding, Grand Opening, Travelling, Moving Engagement, Trading, Signing Contracts, Burial
13	**Sun**	Grand Opening, Signing Contracts, Construction Wedding, Moving, Burial, Travelling, Blessing
14	Mon	Unlucky Day Not Suitable for Important Activities
15	**Tue**	Moving, Stove Set-up, Trading, Construction Wedding, Grand Opening, Travelling
16	Wed	Worship, Capturing
17	Thu	Unlucky Day Not Suitable for Important Activities
18	Fri	Worship, Social Gathering, Decorating
19	**Sat**	Grand Opening, Construction, Money Collecting Travelling, Trading, Net Weaving, Wedding Planting
20	Sun	Worship, Net Weaving

Lucky Hours			Direction of Happiness	Direction of Opportunity	Direction of Wealth
01-03	03-05	13-15	NE	SW	SE
03-05 05-07 15-17 19-21 21-23			NW	SW	SE
01-03 09-11 13-15 15-17 19-21 21-23			SW	W	W
01-03 11-13 13-15 21-23			S	NW	W
01-03 05-07 11-13 13-15 15-17			SE	NE	E
03-05 05-07 11-13 13-15 15-17			NE	SW	N
01-03 13-15 15-17			NW	NE	E
01-03 03-05 05-07 09-11 11-13 15-17 21-23			SW	NE	E
01-03 03-05 05-07 13-15 19-21			S	E	S
03-05 05-07 19-21			SE	E	S

Date	Day	Favourable Activities
Jun 21	*Mon*	Unlucky Day Not Suitable for Important Activities
22	Tue	Decorating, Crack Refilling, Tailoring
23	**Wed**	Worship, Grand Opening, Money Collecting, Moving, Wedding, Tailoring, Door-fixing, Construction
24	**Thu**	Grand Opening, Door-fixing, Construction, Travelling, Tailoring, Money Collecting, Moving, Wedding
25	**Fri**	Grand Opening, Construction, Wedding, Moving, Travelling, Tailoring, Blessing, Decorating
26	*Sat*	Unlucky Day Not Suitable for Important Activities
27	**Sun**	Blessing, Wedding, Signing Contracts, Trading, Travelling, Engagement, Grand Opening, Construction
28	Mon	Worship, Capturing, Bathing, Hair Cutting
29	*Tue*	Unlucky Day Not Suitable for Important Activities
30	Wed	Worship

Lucky Hours			Direction of Happiness	Direction of Opportunity	Direction of Wealth
01-03 03-05 07-09 13-15 21-23			NE	SW	SE
01-03 15-17 19-21			NW	N	SE
09-11 11-13 15-17 19-21 21-23			SW	NW	W
09-11 11-13 13-15 21-23			S	NW	W
01-03 07-09 09-11 13-15 15-17			SE	SW	N
07-09 09-11 11-13 13-15 15-17			NE	SW	N
01-03 11-13 13-15 15-17			NW	SW	E
01-03 03-05 05-07 11-13 13-15 19-21			SW	S	E
01-03 03-05 05-07 07-09 09-11 13-15			S	E	S
01-03 07-09 09-11 15-17 19-21			SE	E	S

Date	Day	Favourable Activities
Jul 1	**Thu**	Animal Acquiring, Start Learning, Trading Signing Contracts, Grand Opening, Construction
2	Fri	Worship, Net Weaving
3	**Sat**	Wedding, Construction, Nursery Set-up, Moving Travelling, Engagement, Bed Set-up
4	Sun	Tailoring, Decorating, Crack Refilling
5	Mon	Worship
6	**Tue**	Trading, Planting, Moving, Signing Contracts Construction, Travelling, House Cleaning
7	**Wed**	Grand Opening, Hair Cutting, Construction Travelling, Blessing, Tailoring, Moving, Burial
8	Thu	Unlucky Day Not Suitable for Important Activities
9	Fri	Worship, Net Weaving, Animal Acquiring Wedding
10	Sat	Hair Cutting, Bathing

Lucky Hours	Direction of Happiness	Direction of Opportunity	Direction of Wealth
03-05 07-09 13-15 19-21	NE	NE	SE
03-05 05-07 13-15 15-17 19-21 21-23	NW	SW	SE
09-11 15-17 21-23	SW	W	W
01-03 09-11 11-13 13-15 19-21	S	W	W
05-07 09-11 13-15 15-17	SE	SW	N
03-05 05-07 09-11 11-13 13-15 15-17	NE	SW	N
01-03 07-09 09-11 11-13 13-15 15-17	NW	SW	E
03-05 07-09 09-11 11-13	SW	NE	E
03-05 05-07 09-11 13-15 19-21 21-23	S	E	S
03-05 05-07 07-09 11-13 19-21 21-23	SE	E	S

Date	Day	Favourable Activities
Jul 11	**Sun**	Wedding, Hair Cutting, Engagement, Blessing Travelling, Construction, Animal Acquiring Burial
12	Mon	Unlucky Day Not Suitable for Important Activities
13	**Tue**	Grand Opening, Engagement, Bed Set-up Net Weaving, Wedding, Trading, Burial
14	**Wed**	Grand Opening, Construction, Wedding Travelling, Moving, Start Learning, Burial
15	Thu	Worship, Hunting, Capturing
16	Fri	Worship, Start Learning
17	Sat	Decorating, Crack Refilling, Burial
18	**Sun**	Blessing, Engagement, Wedding, Travelling Tailoring, Moving
19	Mon	Worship, Blessing, Bathing, House Cleaning
20	Tue	Unlucky Day Not Suitable for Important Activities

Lucky Hours	Direction of Happiness	Direction of Opportunity	Direction of Wealth
23-01 03-05 07-09 13-15 15-17	NE	NE	SE
23-01 03-05 05-07 15-17	NW	N	SE
23-01 05-07 11-13	SW	W	W
03-05 11-13 13-15	S	NW	W
05-07 09-11 13-15 15-17	SE	NE	N
23-01 03-05 11-13 13-15 15-17	NE	SW	N
03-05 11-13 13-15 15-17	NW	SW	E
03-05 05-07 09-11 11-13 15-17	SW	S	E
23-01 05-07 07-09 09-11 13-15	S	E	S
23-01 03-05 07-09 09-11 15-17	SE	SE	S

Date	Day	Favourable Activities
Jul 21	Wed	Worship, Decorating
22	Thu	Signing Contracts, Trading, Start Learning Construction, Tailoring
23	Fri	Capturing, Bathing, Hair Cutting
24	Sat	Unlucky Day Not Suitable for Important Activities
25	Sun	Travelling, Engagement, Tailoring, Trading Grand Opening, Signing Contracts, Bed Set-up
26	Mon	Worship, Grand Opening, Animal Acquiring Wedding, Moving, Planting, Travelling Construction
27	Tue	Worship, Planting, Money Collecting, Capturing
28	Wed	Unlucky Day (Lunar Eclipse) Not Suitable for Important Activities
29	Thu	Net Weaving, Crack Refilling, Burial
30	Fri	Worship, Travelling, Social Gathering, Wedding
31	Sat	Grand Opening, Hair Cutting, Wedding, Moving Construction, Travelling, Engagement, Burial

Lucky Hours			Direction of Happiness	Direction of Opportunity	Direction of Wealth
03-05 05-07 09-11 13-15			NE	NE	SE
23-01 03-05 05-07 13-15			NW	SW	SE
23-01 09-11 19-21 21-23			SW	W	W
23-01 09-11 11-13 21-23			S	NW	W
05-07 07-09 09-11 11-13 13-15			SE	NE	N
23-01 03-05 05-07 11-13 13-15			NE	SW	N
03-05 07-09 09-11 11-13 13-15 21-23			NW	NE	E
03-05 09-11 11-13 13-15 19-21			SW	NE	E
03-05 05-07 09-11 13-15 21-23			S	E	S
23-01 03-05 05-07 09-11 11-13 19-21			SE	E	S
23-01 07-09 09-11 13-15 15-17			NE	SW	SE

Date	Day	Favourable Activities
Aug 1	*Sun*	Unlucky Day Not Suitable for Important Activities
2	Mon	Worship, Net Weaving, Fishing, Hunting
3	**Tue**	Tailoring, Construction, Animal Acquiring Social Gathering, Bathing
4	Wed	Hair Cutting, Bathing, Tailoring, Capturing
5	*Thu*	Unlucky Day Not Suitable for Important Activities
6	**Fri**	Engagement, Grand Opening, Signing Contracts Trading, Planting, Animal Acquiring
7	*Sat*	Unlucky Day Not Suitable for Important Activities
8	**Sun**	Start Learning, Engagement, Animal Acquiring Grand Opening, Burial
9	Mon	Unlucky Day Not Suitable for Important Activities
10	**Tue**	Construction, Bed Set-up, Travelling, Trading Signing Contracts, Wedding, Start Learning Hair Cutting

Lucky Hours			Direction of Happiness	Direction of Opportunity	Direction of Wealth
23-01	03-05	07-09	NW	SW	SE
15-17					
23-01	03-05	05-07	SW	W	W
09-11	15-17	19-21			
21-23					
03-05	11-13	13-15	S	W	W
19-21	21-23				
05-07	07-09	09-11	SE	NE	N
15-17					
23-01	03-05	05-07	NE	N	N
09-11	15-17				
03-05	05-07	07-09	NW	NE	E
03-05	05-07	09-11	SW	NE	E
11-13	19-21				
03-05	05-07	09-11	S	E	S
21-23					
23-01	05-07	07-09	SE	SE	S
09-11	15-17	19-21			
01-03	13-15		NE	SW	SE

Date	Day	Favourable Activities
Aug 11	*Wed*	Unlucky Day (Solar Eclipse) Not Suitable for Important Activities
12	Thu	Travelling, House Cleaning, Animal Acquiring, Burial
13	*Fri*	Unlucky Day Not Suitable for Important Activities
14	**Sat**	Grand Opening, Travelling, Construction Moving, Trading, Animal Acquiring, Burial
15	Sun	Worship, Decorating, Passage-fixing Bathing
16	**Mon**	Blessing, Start Learning, Signing Contracts Grand Opening, Moving, Travelling, Trading Construction
17	Tue	Hunting, Capturing
18	*Wed*	Unlucky Day Not Suitable for Important Activities
19	**Thu**	Blessing, Wedding, Bed Set-up, Travelling Trading, Moving, Signing Contracts, Burial
20	Fri	Worship, Start Learning

Lucky Hours	Direction of Happiness	Direction of Opportunity	Direction of Wealth
23-01 05-07 15-17 19-21 21-23	NW	SW	SE
23-01 01-03 09-11 13-15 15-17 19-21 21-23	SW	W	W
01-03 11-13 13-15 21-23	S	NW	W
01-03 05-07 11-13 13-15 15-17	SE	NE	N
23-01 05-07 11-13 13-15 15-17	NE	SW	N
01-03 13-15 15-17	NW	NE	E
01-03 05-07 09-11 11-13 15-17 21-23	SW	NE	E
01-03 05-07 13-15 19-21	S	E	S
23-01 05-07 19-21	SE	E	S
23-01 01-03 07-09 13-15 21-23	NE	SW	SE

Date	Day	Favourable Activities
Aug 21	**Sat**	Grand Opening, Signing Contracts, Wedding Trading, Net Weaving, Animal Acquiring
22	**Sun**	Worship, Travelling, Construction, Bed Set-up Start Learning, Ditch-digging
23	Mon	Worship, Start Learning
24	**Tue**	Blessing, Hair Cutting, Travelling, Wedding Moving, Burial
25	Wed	Unlucky Day Not Suitable for Important Activities
26	Thu	Planting, Animal Acquiring, Decorating Crack Refilling
27	Fri	Worship, Passage-fixing, Decorating Bathing
28	**Sat**	Travelling, Wedding, Trading, Grand Opening Construction, Moving, Burial
29	**Sun**	Engagement, Construction, Signing Contracts Trading, Travelling, Moving, Grand Opening Burial
30	Mon	Unlucky Day Not Suitable for Important Activities
31	Tue	Worship, Burial

Lucky Hours			Direction of Happiness	Direction of Opportunity	Direction of Wealth
23-01 01-03 15-17 19-21			NW	N	SE
09-11 11-13 15-17 19-21 21-23			SW	NW	W
09-11 11-13 13-15 21-23			S	NW	W
01-03 07-09 09-11 13-15 15-17			SE	SW	N
23-01 07-09 09-11 11-13 13-15 15-17			NE	SW	N
01-03 11-13 13-15 15-17			NW	SW	E
01-03 05-07 11-13 13-15 19-21			SW	S	E
23-01 01-03 05-07 07-09 09-11 13-15			S	E	S
23-01 01-03 07-09 09-11 15-17 19-21			SE	E	S
05-07 07-09 13-15 19-21			NE	NE	SE
05-07 13-15 15-17 19-21 21-23			NW	SW	SE

Date	Day	Favourable Activities
Sep 1	Wed	Worship, Start Learning, Engagement
2	**Thu**	Signing Contracts, Engagement, Trading Wedding, Grand Opening, Moving
3	**Fri**	Blessing, Grand Opening, Engagement, Moving Start Learning, Construction, Wedding Ditch-digging
4	Sat	Construction, Decorating, Crack Refilling
5	Sun	Travelling, House Cleaning, Animal Acquiring, Bathing
6	Mon	Unlucky Day Not Suitable for Important Activities
7	**Tue**	Wedding, Construction, Grand Opening, Moving Net Weaving, Animal Acquiring, Planting, Burial
8	Wed	Worship, Bed Set-up, Bathing, Travelling
9	Thu	Worship, Travelling, House Cleaning, Bathing
10	**Fri**	Grand Opening, Trading, Engagement, Wedding Signing Contracts, Travelling, Construction Burial

Lucky Hours			Direction of Happiness	Direction of Opportunity	Direction of Wealth
09-11	15-17	21-23	SW	W	W
01-03 09-11 11-13 13-15 19-21			S	W	W
05-07 09-11 13-15 15-17			SE	SW	N
05-07 09-11 11-13 13-15 15-17			NE	SW	N
01-03 07-09 09-11 11-13 13-15 15-17			NW	SW	S
07-09	09-11	11-13	SW	NE	E
05-07 09-11 13-15 19-21 21-23			S	E	S
05-07 07-09 11-13 19-21 21-23			SE	E	S
23-01 01-03 03-05 07-09 13-15 15-17			NE	NE	SE
23-01 01-03 03-05 15-17			NW	N	SE

Date	Day	Favourable Activities
Sep 11	Sat	Engagement, Capturing, Door-fixing, Burial
12	Sun	Unlucky Day Not Suitable for Important Activities
13	Mon	Start Learning, Moving, Wedding, Trading Stove Set-up, Bed Set-up
14	Tue	Grand Opening, Animal Acquiring, Construction Start Learning, Moving, Wedding, Trading Blessing
15	Wed	Worship, Capturing
16	Thu	Blessing, Start Learning, Travelling, Wedding Moving, Tailoring
17	Fri	Planting, Hair Cutting, Decorating Crack Refilling, Burial
18	Sat	Unlucky Day Not Suitable for Important Activities
19	Sun	Hair Cutting, House Cleaning, Planting Travelling
20	Mon	Grand Opening, Moving, Net Weaving, Trading Construction, Crack Refilling, Decorating Travelling

Lucky Hours	Direction of Happiness	Direction of Opportunity	Direction of Wealth
23-01 11-13	SW	W	W
03-05 11-13 13-15	S	NW	W
01-03 09-11 13-15 15-17	SE	NE	N
23-01 03-05 11-13 13-15 15-17	NE	SW	N
01-03 03-05 11-13 13-15 15-17	NW	SW	E
03-05 09-11 11-13 15-17	SW	S	E
23-01 01-03 07-09 09-11 13-15	S	E	S
23-01 01-03 03-05 07-09 09-11 15-17	SE	SE	S
01-03 03-05 09-11 13-15	NE	NE	SE
23-01 01-03 03-05 13-15	NW	SW	SE

Date	Day	Favourable Activities
Sep 21	Tue	Worship, Decorating, Passage-fixing Bathing
22	Wed	Unlucky Day Not Suitable for Important Activities
23	Thu	Capturing, Stove Set-up, Hair Cutting, Bathing
24	Fri	Unlucky Day Not Suitable for Important Activities
25	Sat	Blessing, Travelling, Moving, Grand Opening Wedding, Bed Set-up, Trading, Burial
26	Sun	Grand Opening, Worship, Trading, Construction Start Learning, Moving, Engagement, Wedding
27	Mon	Worship, Capturing
28	Tue	Blessing, Social Gathering, Travelling, Wedding Engagement, Animal Acquiring, Start Learning
29	Wed	Tailoring, Hair Cutting, Planting, Burial
30	Thu	Unlucky Day Not Suitable for Important Activities

Lucky Hours	Direction of Happiness	Direction of Opportunity	Direction of Wealth
23-01 01-03 09-11 19-21 21-23	SW	W	W
23-01 09-11 11-13 21-23	S	NW	W
01-03 07-09 09-11 11-13 13-15	SE	NE	N
23-01 03-05 11-13 13-15	NE	SW	N
01-03 03-05 07-09 09-11 11-13 13-15 21-23	NW	NE	E
01-03 03-05 09-11 11-13 13-15 19-21	SW	NE	E
01-03 03-05 09-11 13-15 21-23	S	E	S
23-01 03-05 09-11 11-13 19-21	SE	E	S
23-01 01-03 07-09 09-11 13-15 15-17	NE	SW	SE
23-01 01-03 03-05 07-09 15-17	NW	SW	SE

Date	Day	Favourable Activities
Oct 1	Fri	Hair Cutting, Bathing, House Cleaning Travelling
2	**Sat**	Travelling, Moving, Grand Opening, Trading Signing Contracts, Money Collecting
3	Sun	Worship, Passage-fixing, Decorating Bathing
4	**Mon**	Social Gathering, Construction, Signing Contracts Wedding, Engagement, Animal Acquiring Trading
5	Tue	Capturing, Bathing, Hair Cutting
6	*Wed*	Unlucky Day Not Suitable for Important Activities
7	Thu	Worship, Blessing, Tailoring
8	*Fri*	Unlucky Day Not Suitable for Important Activities
9	**Sat**	Wedding, Grand Opening, Trading, Construction Engagement, Travelling, Start Learning, Burial
10	Sun	Worship, Stove Set-up, Capturing, Hunting

Lucky Hours			Direction of Happiness	Direction of Opportunity	Direction of Wealth
23-01	03-05	09-11	SW	W	W
15-17	19-21	21-23			
01-03	03-05	11-13	S	W	W
13-15	19-21	21-23			
01-03	07-09	09-11	SE	NE	N
15-17					
23-01	03-05	09-11	NE	N	N
15-17					
01-03	03-05	07-09	NW	NE	E
03-05	09-11	11-13	SW	NE	E
19-21					
01-03	03-05	09-11	S	E	S
21-23					
23-01	07-09	09-11	SE	SE	S
15-17	19-21				
01-03	03-05	13-15	NE	SW	SE
23-01	03-05	05-07	NW	SW	SE
15-17	19-21	21-23			

Date	Day	Favourable Activities
Oct 11	**Mon**	Grand Opening, Start Learning, Wedding Travelling, Construction, Nursery Set-up Engagement, Ditch-digging
12	Tue	Unlucky Day Not Suitable for Important Activities
13	Wed	House Cleaning
14	Thu	Hair Cutting, House Cleaning, Grand Opening Bathing
15	Fri	Worship, Start Learning, Bathing
16	Sat	Worship, Passage-fixing
17	Sun	Net Weaving
18	**Mon**	Net Weaving, Animal Acquiring, Construction Travelling, Moving, Planting, Wedding, Burial
19	Tue	Unlucky Day Not Suitable for Important Activities
20	Wed	Worship, Bed Set-up, Tailoring, Hunting

Lucky Hours			Direction of Happiness	Direction of Opportunity	Direction of Wealth
23-01	01-03	09-11	SW	W	W
13-15	15-17	19-21			
21-23					
01-03	11-13	13-15	S	NW	W
21-23					
01-03	05-07	11-13	SE	NE	N
13-15	15-17				
23-01	03-05	05-07	NE	SW	N
11-13	13-15	15-17			
01-03	13-15	15-17	NW	NE	E
01-03	03-05	05-07	SW	NE	E
09-11	11-13	15-17			
21-23					
01-03	03-05	05-07	S	E	S
13-15	19-21				
23-01	03-05	05-07	SE	E	S
19-21					
23-01	01-03	03-05	NE	SW	SE
13-15	21-23				
23-01	01-03	15-17	NW	N	SE
19-21					

Date	Day	Favourable Activities
Oct 21	**Thu**	Signing Contracts, Start Learning, Construction Moving, Trading, Grand Opening, Wedding Burial
22	Fri	Hunting, Capturing
23	**Sat**	Grand Opening, Start Learning, Moving Engagement, Travelling, Ditch-digging, Wedding Construction
24	Sun	Unlucky Day Not Suitable for Important Activities
25	**Mon**	Worship, Moving, Animal Acquiring, Travelling Money Collecting, Tailoring
26	**Tue**	Start Learning, House Cleaning, Hair Cutting Animal Acquiring, Money Collecting, Moving Blessing, Travelling
27	Wed	Worship, Travelling, Bathing, Burial
28	Thu	Passage-fixing
29	Fri	Burial
30	Sat	Worship, Bathing, Bed Set-up, Door-fixing
31	Sun	Unlucky Day Not Suitable for Important Activities

Lucky Hours			Direction of Happiness	Direction of Opportunity	Direction of Wealth
09-11 11-13 15-17 19-21 21-23			SW	NW	W
09-11 11-13 13-15 21-23			S	NW	W
01-03 09-11 13-15 15-17			SE	SW	N
23-01 09-11 11-13 13-15 15-17			NE	SW	N
01-03 11-13 13-15 15-17			NW	SW	E
01-03 03-05 05-07 11-13 13-15 19-21			SW	S	E
23-01 01-03 03-05 05-07 09-11 13-15			S	E	S
23-01 01-03 09-11 15-17 19-21			SE	E	S
03-05 13-15 19-21			NE	NE	SE
03-05 05-07 13-15 15-17 19-21 21-23			NW	SW	SE
09-11 15-17 21-23			SW	W	W

Date	Day	Favourable Activities
Nov 1	Mon	Worship, Bed Set-up, Hunting
2	**Tue**	Start Learning, Social Gathering, Grand Opening Travelling, Moving, Engagement, Wedding
3	Wed	Hunting, Capturing
4	**Thu**	Blessing, Ditch-digging, Travelling, Grand Opening Nursery Set-up, Moving, Start Learning
5	Fri	Unlucky Day Not Suitable for Important Activities
6	**Sat**	Moving, Social Gathering, Animal Acquiring Engagement, Travelling
7	Sun	Unlucky Day Not Suitable for Important Activities
8	**Mon**	Moving, Hair Cutting, Trading, Wedding Construction, Engagement, Travelling, Burial
9	Tue	Worship, Crack Refilling
10	**Wed**	Signing Contracts, Construction, Grand Opening Travelling, Trading, Wedding, Burial

Lucky Hours	Direction of Happiness	Direction of Opportunity	Direction of Wealth
01-03 09-11 11-13 13-15 19-21	S	W	W
05-07 09-11 13-15 15-17	SE	SW	N
03-05 05-07 09-11 11-13 13-15 15-17	NE	SW	N
01-03 09-11 11-13 13-15 15-17	NW	SW	E
03-05 09-11 11-13	SW	NE	E
03-05 05-07 09-11 13-15 19-21 21-23	S	E	S
03-05 05-07 11-13 19-21 21-23	SE	E	S
23-01 01-03 03-05 07-09 13-15 15-17	NE	NE	SE
23-01 01-03 03-05 05-07 15-17	NW	N	SE
23-01 05-07 11-13	SW	W	W

Date	Day	Favourable Activities
Nov 11	**Thu**	Engagement, Travelling, Moving, Trading Wedding, Grand Opening, Construction
12	**Fri**	Worship, Capturing, Hunting, Start Learning Hair Cutting, Bathing
13	*Sat*	Unlucky Day Not Suitable for Important Activities
14	**Sun**	Grand Opening, Moving, Wedding, Construction Bed Set-up, Travelling, Engagement, Burial
15	**Mon**	Blessing, Tailoring, Engagement, Trading Grand Opening, Construction, Signing Contracts
16	Tue	House Cleaning, Bathing, Capturing
17	*Wed*	Unlucky Day Not Suitable for Important Activities
18	Thu	Worship
19	Fri	Worship, Bathing
20	**Sat**	Travelling, Moving, House Cleaning, Bathing Hair Cutting, Engagement

Lucky Hours			Direction of Happiness	Direction of Opportunity	Direction of Wealth
03-05	11-13	13-15	S	NW	W
01-03 05-07 13-15 15-17			SE	NE	N
23-01 03-05 11-13 13-15 15-17			NE	SW	N
01-03 03-05 11-13 13-15 15-17			NW	SW	E
03-05 05-07 11-13 15-17			SW	S	E
23-01 01-03 05-07 07-09 13-15			S	E	S
23-01 01-03 03-05 07-09 15-17			SE	SE	S
01-03 03-05 05-07 13-15			NE	NE	SE
23-01 01-03 03-05 05-07 13-15			NW	SW	SE
23-01 01-03 19-21 21-23			SW	W	W

Date	Day	Favourable Activities
Nov 21	Sun	Worship
22	**Mon**	Grand Opening, Trading, Wedding, Engagement Burial
23	**Tue**	Construction, Blessing, Travelling, Moving Wedding, Grand Opening, Trading, Burial
24	**Wed**	Worship, Wedding, Tailoring, Animal Acquiring Engagement, Hair Cutting, Burial
25	Thu	Unlucky Day Not Suitable for Important Activities
26	Fri	Worship, Tailoring, Hunting
27	**Sat**	Start Learning, Grand Opening, Construction Bed Set-up, Engagement, Trading
28	**Sun**	Wedding, Travelling, Tailoring, Construction Moving, Planting, Social Gathering, Burial
29	Mon	Unlucky Day Not Suitable for Important Activities
30	Tue	Tailoring, Weaving

Lucky Hours			Direction of Happiness	Direction of Opportunity	Direction of Wealth
23-01 11-13 21-23			S	NW	W
01-03 05-07 07-09 11-13 13-15			SE	NE	N
23-01 03-05 05-07 11-13 13-15			NE	SW	N
01-03 03-05 07-09 11-13 13-15 21-23			NW	NE	E
01-03 03-05 11-13 13-15 19-21			SW	NE	E
01-03 03-05 05-07 13-15 21-23			S	E	S
23-01 03-05 05-07 11-13 19-21			SE	E	S
23-01 01-03 07-09 13-15 15-17			NE	SW	SE
23-01 01-03 03-05 07-09 15-17			NW	SW	SE
23-01 03-05 05-07 15-17 19-21 21-23			SW	W	W

Date	Day	Favourable Activities
Dec 1	Wed	Worship, Bathing
2	Thu	Travelling, Start Learning, House Cleaning Construction
3	Fri	Worship, Social Gathering, Decorating Crack Refilling
4	**Sat**	Grand Opening, Engagement, Wedding, Trading Travelling, Construction, Moving, Burial
5	**Sun**	Wedding, Trading, Signing Contracts, Moving Travelling, Grand Opening, Engagement
6	Mon	Hair Cutting, Net Weaving, Capturing, Hunting
7	Tue	Unlucky Day Not Suitable for Important Activities
8	Wed	Unlucky Day Not Suitable for Important Activities
9	Thu	Worship, Hunting, Ditch-digging
10	**Fri**	Start Learning, Grand Opening, Signing Contracts Wedding, Trading, Travelling, Moving, Burial

Lucky Hours			Direction of Happiness	Direction of Opportunity	Direction of Wealth
01-03	03-05	11-13	S	W	W
13-15	19-21	21-23			
01-03	05-07	07-09	SE	NE	N
15-17					
23-01	03-05	05-07	NE	N	N
15-17					
01-03	03-05	05-07	NW	NE	E
07-09					
03-05	05-07	11-13	SW	NE	E
19-21					
01-03	03-05	05-07	S	E	S
21-23					
23-01	05-07	07-09	SE	SE	S
15-17	19-21				
01-03	03-05	13-15	NE	SW	SE
23-01	03-05	05-07	NW	SW	SE
15-17	19-21	21-23			
23-01	01-03	09-11	SW	W	W
13-15	15-17	19-21			
21-23					

Date	Day	Favourable Activities
Dec 11	*Sat*	Unlucky Day Not Suitable for Important Activities
12	**Sun**	Construction, Nursery Set-up, Tailoring Ditch-digging, Start Learning
13	Mon	Bathing, Crack Refilling
14	Tue	Worship, Decorating
15	**Wed**	Trading, Money Collecting, House Cleaning Tailoring, Wedding, Travelling, Engagement Burial
16	**Thu**	Grand Opening, Start Learning, Trading Travelling, Construction, Wedding, Burial
17	Fri	Decorating, Passage-fixing
18	**Sat**	Blessing, Wedding, Travelling, Animal Acquiring Trading, Construction, Moving, Engagement
19	Sun	Worship, Capturing
20	Mon	Unlucky Day Not Suitable for Important Activities

Lucky Hours	Direction of Happiness	Direction of Opportunity	Direction of Wealth
01-03 13-15 21-23	S	NW	W
01-03 05-07 13-15 15-17	SE	NE	N
23-01 03-05 05-07 13-15 15-17	NE	SW	N
01-03 13-15 15-17	NW	NE	E
01-03 03-05 05-07 09-11 15-17 21-23	SW	NE	E
01-03 03-05 05-07 13-15 19-21	S	E	S
23-01 03-05 05-07 19-21	SE	E	S
23-01 01-03 03-05 07-09 13-15 21-23	NE	SW	SE
23-01 01-03 15-17 19-21	NW	N	SE
09-11 15-17 19-21 21-23	SW	NW	W

Date	Day	Favourable Activities
Dec 21	*Tue*	Unlucky Day Not Suitable for Important Activities
22	**Wed**	Travelling, Moving, Grand Opening, Wedding Hair Cutting, Start Learning, Trading
23	*Thu*	Unlucky Day Not Suitable for Important Activities
24	**Fri**	Blessing, Construction, Planting, Ditch-digging Start Learning, Nursery Set-up
25	Sat	Decorating, Crack Refilling, Tailoring
26	Sun	Worship, Decorating
27	**Mon**	Wedding, Grand Opening, Trading, Moving Travelling, Hair Cutting, Construction
28	**Tue**	Grand Opening, Money Collecting, Trading Signing Contracts, Construction, Nursery Set-up Net Weaving, Planting
29	Wed	Decorating, Passage-fixing
30	**Thu**	Net Weaving, Door-fixing, Wedding, Tailoring Engagement, Trading, Construction
31	Fri	Worship, Capturing

Lucky Hours	Direction of Happiness	Direction of Opportunity	Direction of Wealth
09-11 13-15 21-23	S	NW	W
01-03 07-09 09-11 13-15 15-17	SE	SW	N
23-01 07-09 09-11 13-15 15-17	NE	SW	N
01-03 13-15 15-17	NW	SW	E
01-03 03-05 05-07 13-15 19-21	SW	S	E
23-01 01-03 03-05 05-07 07-09 09-11 13-15	S	E	S
23-01 01-03 07-09 09-11 15-17 19-21	SE	E	S
03-05 07-09 13-15 19-21	NE	NE	SE
03-05 05-07 13-15 15-17 19-21 21-23	NW	SW	SE
09-11 15-17 21-23	SW	W	W
01-03 09-11 13-15 19-21	S	W	W

Factors Influencing Chinese
Astrological Predictions:

The

Lucky and
Unlucky Stars

Much has been written about Chinese Astrology and the
12 related animal lunar signs. This chapter attempts to
clarify the factors, both good and bad, which influence
the Lunar Signs in 1999, the Year of the Rabbit.

Over many years spent researching ancient textbooks on
Chinese Astrology, most of which have never been translated into
English, I have developed this system with the hope of sharing
the information in a distilled and easy-to-understand manner.
Chinese Astrology can be compared to Western Astrology. Simply,
in Western Astrology, the Stars and their specific positioning to the
sun relates profoundly to the characterization of each sun Sign.
This is individualized by the time and place of birth. Thereafter,
annual predictions, based on the same criteria, are made. In the
case of Chinese Astrology the factors relating to predictions
include positioning of the Stars to the moon, plus time and place
of birth. It is the year which signifies the Sign.

The characterization of predictions based on Chinese Astrology
can be referred to as heavenly luck. In the Chinese system, however,
this heavenly luck can be influenced by the practice of Feng Shui,

thus manifesting earthly luck. Feng Shui provides a balance of power, much as Yin and Yang, light and dark, masculine and feminine, passive and active, and the sun and the moon are the forces that keep the world and each one of us in tune with life. So too can we balance heavenly luck and earthly luck.

As you read through the specific Signs you will notice that there are many more Unlucky Stars than Lucky Stars. The ancient Chinese believed it was better to know more about impending bad luck than good. So this is simply a warning system, and therefore what at first may appear negative can be turned into a positive. Chinese soothsayers believe that through the art of Feng Shui, the art of placement and direction, each individual can enhance his or her good luck and minimize bad luck. I will show you how to counteract any bad luck in the chapter relating to your particular Chinese Horoscope Sign.

Stars Influencing the Chinese Horoscope in 1999

The Lucky Stars
Blessing Virtue

When this Star appears, people will enjoy a year full of blessings from other people. Its message is that it is best to set a good example and be kind to those who have been helpful in the past. By following the practice of 'one good turn deserves another', blessings will manifest continually.

Commander's Saddle

In ancient China, military commanders fought their battles on horseback. In battle a good saddle was essential for brave and effective fighting. As a result, the idea of a commander's saddle came to symbolize courage and military superiority.

Should this Star appear in your horoscope you can conquer life's obstacles if you are courageous enough. However, remember to be merciful towards your defeated enemies.

Crape Myrtle

Since the flower, 'Crape Myrtle' was deliberately planted inside the royal courts of the Forbidden City, it became known as the Emperor's Flower. Later, it came to symbolize superiority within the feudal hierarchy.

People under this Star will easily get large promotions, and will have the authority and confidence to overcome all difficulties and opposition they may face.

Dragon's Virtue

Virtue was highly appreciated by Confucius. The ancient Chinese believed that virtue not only set a good example to others, but provided its own good results. Of the four 'Virtue' Stars in the Chinese Horoscope, 'Dragon's Virtue' is one of the most important.

Since for centuries the dragon was regarded as a symbol of the Emperor, the 'Dragon's Virtue' signified the Emperor's virtue and goodness, which would benefit the entire empire and its people.

When this Star appears, people will have a successful and productive year. They will get support from other people, especially their subordinates.

Earthly Salvation

There are three 'Salvation' Stars in the Chinese Horoscope: 'Heavenly Salvation', 'Earthly Salvation', and 'God of Salvation'. They are all considered to have the power to help people out of troubles and disasters. Among the three, 'Earthly Salvation' is the least important. Still, its appearance is a good omen for those in trouble.

When this Star appears, people's suffering will be alleviated. Nonetheless, people should still try to keep themselves out of difficulty, since the Star's influence is limited.

The Eight Chiefs

In the traditional Chinese ruling hierarchy, eight chiefs helped the emperor to govern the whole country. Although theoretically under the three prime ministers, they nonetheless had enough authority to keep everything in order.

When this Star appears, people will be promoted and possess the power to rule, and to scare off any challengers.

God of Salvation

Ancient Chinese peasants often led a precarious existence, vulnerable as they were to threats such as wars, floods, droughts and famines. However, they believed that in critical times the God of Salvation would protect them from total destruction.

There are three 'Salvation' Stars in the Chinese Horoscope, of which this is considered to be the most powerful. It is generally regarded as having the power to suppress negative influences from any Unlucky Stars within the same Sign.

God of Study and Career

The Chinese regard this Star as strongly influencing one's academic and career achievements. Traditionally, all young Chinese students would go to the temple to worship this Star, and ask for its blessing on their next Civil Service Exam.

The appearance of this Star is a very good omen. People will have a very successful and productive year – even more so if they work hard. Extra effort will translate into significantly greater rewards.

Heavenly Happiness

The Chinese have always considered marriage to be one of the greatest blessings in life. It not only brings the joys of family life, but also helps to perpetuate the family, hopefully for generations to come. Such a gift is considered to be heaven-sent. Similarly, this Star symbolizes marital happiness and is highly regarded in the Chinese Horoscope.

When this Star appears, its presence signifies romance, a healing of broken relationships, and possibly even marriage before the year is out.

Heavenly Salvation

'Heavenly Salvation' is another of the three Salvation Stars, which assist people in getting out of problems and disasters. Its appearance is a good omen.

When this Star appears, stick to what you believe in and do not give up, even if the situation appears impossible. When most needed you will get crucial assistance leading to a breakthrough.

Heavenly Virtue

Virtue was highly appreciated by Confucius, the great Chinese philosopher. The ancient Chinese believed that virtue not only set a good example to others, but provided its own benefits and rewards as well. The Chinese Horoscope has four 'Virtue' Stars, with Heavenly Virtue being the most influential.

The appearance of this Star is definitely a very good omen. It minimizes negative influences from the Unlucky Stars, and bestows a peaceful and joyful year.

Jade Hall

In ancient China, thousands and thousands of scholars prepared for the Government Examinations. However, only a few hundred of them ever passed and would consequently be admitted to the ruling class. This newly-promoted elite would be deeply honoured with a big feast in a large decorated jade hall to show off their brilliant success.

When this Star appears, you will do well in your studies and in your work. You will have an important breakthrough if you work at it.

Lunar Virtue

Virtue was highly appreciated by Confucius. The ancient Chinese believed that virtue not only set a good example for others to follow, but also produced its own rewards. Lunar Virtue is the least important of the four 'Virtue' Stars in the Chinese Horoscope, but is especially favourable for females.

When this Star appears, people will have enhanced persuasive skills, which can help them achieve important breakthroughs. However, this Star is usually not strong enough to overcome a combination of several Unlucky Stars appearing together within the same Sign.

The Moon

The concept of Yin (female) and Yang (male) is very strong in Chinese culture. Just as the Sun symbolized Yang, the Moon for centuries has symbolized Yin.

The appearance of this Star is a good omen because it will brighten up the world at night.

Pink Phoenix

In traditional Chinese culture the Phoenix was a legendary, mystical bird, famous for spending time in romantic, affectionate pairs. Over time it came to symbolize love and marriage, and for centuries it has been included in Chinese wedding ceremonies.

The appearance of this Star is a very good omen. It indicates a romantic year with good marriage possibilities.

Star of Blessing

During Chinese New Year it is customary to decorate the home with a prominent red banner on which the Chinese character for 'Blessing' is printed, in hopes of bringing good luck. Similarly, in the Chinese Horoscope the presence of the Star of Blessing is considered to be most lucky.

This Star indicates a very fortunate year. It can even change bad luck to good.

The Star of Commander

Although the ancient Chinese loved peace, they also respected their local military commander, who was there to protect them from foreign enemies. A courageous and responsible commander signified a guardian of the peace, and protection from suffering.

The appearance of this Star is a very good omen. It will not only enrich a Sign's luck, but will also minimize negative influences from Unlucky Stars.

The Sun

The concept of Yin (female) and Yang (male) was essential in ancient Chinese culture. The Sun, representing energy and authority, is considered to be the most influential and important Yang symbol, similar to the god Apollo in Greek mythology.

When this Star appears in your horoscope, evil things diminish just like snow melting under the warm sun.

The Three Pillars

In ancient China the *Ding* was a large and heavy cooking pot supported by three strong legs. As *Ding* has been used to symbolize the government, the three legs have symbolized the three prime ministers of the government, who worked as the solid support of the whole country. These ministers possessed the absolute power to keep everything under control.

The appearance of this Star appear in your horoscope is a very good omen. It indicates that you will have enough confidence and strength to overcome opposition and challengers, and can triumph if you commit yourself to your goals.

Travelling Horse

In ancient China travelling on horseback was the fastest and easiest way to get around. So, not surprisingly, the horse came to symbolize travel. Whether the journey would be smooth or not depended on the quality and condition of the horse.

When this Star appears, it indicates that it is a good year to travel for both business and pleasure.

Unity is important for success. In the Chinese Horoscope, this Star harmonizes well with the year. Its appearance is a very good omen.

When this Star appears within your Sign, you will be very popular and find it easy to win the friendship and support of those around you. Such good relations will bring handsome rewards in different projects and investments.

The Unlucky Stars
Black Cloud

Just as black clouds gather before a heavy rainstorm, imaginary black clouds, the ancient Chinese believed, gathered just before the outbreak of disaster. Chinese fortune-tellers would look for these 'black clouds' in face- or palm-reading. When they appeared, it was said life would become less clear, and people would easily lose their way.

The appearance of this Star means that people must maintain a keen perspective on what is happening, or they will not be able to find their way out of disputes. During this period it is important to save money and energy for unexpected 'thunderstorms'.

Bloody Knife

Knives, and other deadly weapons, were not commonly welcomed by the ancient Chinese, who preferred to live in peace. Similarly, a bloody knife was definitely a very bad omen associated with violence and killing.

When this Star appears, it is important to maintain one's temper, and avoid quarrels and fights, which will only bring unpleasant consequences.

Broken Down

The ancient Chinese had little regard for objects that were not whole and contained cracks. In a similar way, a broken soul was much depreciated.

The appearance of this Star is a bad omen. People should be

very careful in protecting their belongings and personal safety, especially when it comes to preventing injurious falls.

Conflict of the Year

Since the ancient Chinese valued harmony, they would try to minimize conflicts quickly, as soon as they broke out. Because this Star signifies conflict, it is not regarded as a good omen.

If this Star appears within your sign, you have to try your best to settle all disputes and conflicts before they get out of hand. Otherwise you will face a lot of problems and your work will be compromised as a result.

Deadly Spell

In ancient times, Chinese magic spells were created through special symbols and characters written by Taoist priests in red ink or even blood. Based on this, the concept of five 'Magic Spell' Stars in the Chinese Horoscope developed.

The most serious Star of all is the 'Deadly Spell'. The ancient Chinese believed that shortly before a person's death the Ruler of Hell would send an invisible 'Deadly Spell' as a summons to the afterlife.

When this Star appears, people have to be very careful about their health and safety, to avoid serious illness, injury, or even death.

Decorative Top

In ancient China, only the nobles and important people were allowed to cover the tops of their carriages with rich decoration, which varied according to rank. Such decorated carriages naturally became associated with high social status, luxury and, interestingly enough, with a certain degree of isolation typical of those who inhabit their own exclusive world away from the masses.

Thus, the implications of this Star are ambiguous. On one hand, when this Star appears people will enjoy a successful year; on the other, they will have a tendency to become isolated if they do not remain connected in their personal relationships.

Dog of Heaven

In Chinese mythology a big, fierce dog would come to threaten and eat people who had done bad deeds. Chinese mythology teaches that this creature causes the eclipse of the sun and moon, by swallowing either sphere. During eclipses, the people would bang cymbals or other metal objects to scare the dog and make him spit out the sun or the moon, thus ending the eclipse.

When this Star appears, people need to stand strong and fight their opponents or they will be swallowed up too.

Earthly Threat

The ancient Chinese believed that malevolent spirits brought dangers and problems into their daily lives. Of these, 'Earthly Threat' was considered to be the least dangerous and damaging of the four 'Threats' in the Chinese Horoscope.

When this Star appears, people should be extra careful about road safety.

Fierce Hercules

Fei Lian is the name of a famous Chinese Hercules who served the wicked Emperor Zhou of the Shang Dynasty. This Emperor's hot temper and tremendous power brought considerable destruction to his people. To live in peace they tried to keep out of his way and not irritate him.

The appearance of this Star is a bad omen. People will be seriously hurt physically and financially if they provoke their superiors.

Five Ghosts

The Chinese believe that ghosts are best avoided since they threaten people's health and safety. To living people, meeting five ghosts at once would definitely be a horrible experience. Surely, then, this Star is not a good omen.

The appearance of this Star is a warning to people to play it safe. Avoid provoking anyone in a position of authority, or it could lead to an endless nightmare.

Floating Up and Down

The Chinese have always suffered from the periodic flooding of the Yellow River, the so-called 'Sorrow of China'. They know from experience how dangerous it is to be caught and be floating up and down in the surging current of a flooding river.

Similarly, when this Star appears, people need to stay alert during this rough year so that they won't be carried away by the swift currents, or even drowned.

Flying Spell

In ancient times, Chinese magic spells were created through special symbols and characters written by Taoist priests in red ink or even blood. Based on this, the concept of five 'Magic Spell' Stars in the Chinese Horoscope developed. This is one of them.

As its name suggests, the 'Flying Spell' is the kind that flew through the sky. When someone experienced bad luck it was blamed on an unfortunate encounter with such a flying spell.

When this Star appears, people should try to keep a low profile and be alert to prepare for unexpected troubles or even accidents.

Funeral Guest

When attending funerals in ancient China it was customary (as it is in the West) to wear black as a symbol of sadness and sobriety. Wearing red or other bright colours showed a lack of respect, and was forbidden on such sombre occasions.

This Star's appearance is a very bad omen, indicating the possibility of death among family and friends. Take extra care of older family members or anyone else who might be in danger.

Funeral Robe

During traditional Chinese funerals, people would wear roughly-tailored yellow hemp clothes as a symbol of their grief, showing they were too overwhelmed with sorrow to worry about finery. Since then these yellow robes have come to symbolize funerals.

The appearance of this Star is not a good omen. It signifies that you need to be alert for potential medical problems among older family members – periodic medical check-ups and, if necessary, effective treatment, should be undertaken regularly.

Funeral's Door

In ancient China funeral ceremonies were held at home. A pair of white lanterns were hung outside to announce the death. The front door was kept closed to prevent unnecessary disturbances by those unconnected with the funeral. Since then, a tightly closed door with a pair of white lanterns has symbolized a grief-stricken family.

When this Star appears, people have to take care of their elderly family members by making sure that they receive the proper medical treatments when required. In addition, they should pay more attention to their home safety.

Gaol House

Going through the judicial system was often a nightmare for the ancient Chinese. They would rather have died than have to go to prison.

When this Star appears, people will have a tendency to get in trouble with the law. It is best to stay on the straight and narrow and avoid anything that causes trouble. Keep in mind that 'it is better to be a hungry bird in the forest than a well-fed bird in a cage'.

The God of Death

This is definitely the least propitious Star in the Chinese Horoscope. It is named after Wang Shen, the God of Death, who the ancient Chinese believed had control over a person's mortality.

The Star's appearance is a very bad omen, a warning to take extreme care, avoid risks, and always follow the motto 'safety first'.

God of Loneliness

In traditional Chinese society, living happily and harmoniously with other family members was considered to be a great blessing.

On the other hand, to live alone or to be ostracized by family or society was considered the most horrible fate. Not surprisingly, this Star is one of the most unpopular in the Chinese Horoscope.

When this Star appears, people need to work on improving their relations with relatives, friends and colleagues, or they may be isolated.

Gradual Drain

Farming has been the major source of income for Chinese peasants for centuries. Because water is essential for irrigation, it has come to symbolize wealth. Over the centuries, Chinese peasants have worked to prevent drainage from their cultivated lands.

Similarly, when this Star appears people need to watch their expenditure and keep within their budget. They should also avoid risky investments and gambling, which could easily lead to financial ruin.

Heavenly Hazards

The ancient Chinese believed that the gods in heaven would deliberately confront people with difficult obstacles in life to test them. Those who failed to pass these dangerous tests, it was believed, would be given a miserable life. Not surprisingly, this Star is considered to be a bad omen.

When this Star appears, people will face many challenges, which they must overcome if they want to avoid losing out.

Heavenly Threat

The ancient Chinese believed that malevolent spirits brought dangers and problems into their daily lives. Of these, 'Heavenly Threat' was considered to be the most dangerous of all, and able to cause serious damage.

The appearance of this Star is a warning to be more careful. Watch out for potential dangers and traps. Follow a conservative, defensive strategy.

Heavenly Weeping

The ancient Chinese believed that Heaven was capable of reacting to and being sensitive towards the experiences and plight of those on earth. If the people suffered from starvation and violence, then Heaven would weep for them. Thus, the appearance of 'Heavenly Weeping' indicates troubles.

When this Star appears, people will face a lot of problems and will have to struggle hard to get out from under them.

Hooked and Strained

Being hooked by sharp objects or strained by ropes is definitely a very terrible experience. Unfortunately, this Star is somewhat related with these two terrible experiences.

The appearance of this Star is a bad omen. Be very careful about every step of the way in order to avoid risking your life within the year.

Huge Drain

The ancient Chinese considered water to be the symbol of wealth, since it was essential for agriculture, the backbone of their economy. On a farm, a failure to manage water could easily lead to dried-out crops, spelling disaster.

This Star's appearance is a warning that a large and sudden financial loss is on the horizon.

Illness Spell

Chinese magical spells were created by Taoist priests, who would write special symbols in red ink or blood on pieces of cloth or paper.

In ancient China staying healthy was a constant struggle due to the generally poor state of medicine and living conditions in the villages. When someone became sick it was believed to have been caused by an evil 'Illness Spell' which had entered their home.

When this Star appears people should protect themselves and their family by being extra careful about diet and hygiene.

Iron Bars

In the Chinese Horoscope the Stars 'Iron Bars' and 'Gaol House' are similar to each other in that they both deal with confinement and punishment for a crime. However, 'Iron Bars' is not as serious as 'Gaol House', since the former refers to a place of temporary detention, while the latter is more like a maximum security prison where few get out.

When this Star appears, you should be careful not to break the law – or be prepared to suffer the consequences.

Isolated Living

For the Chinese, living away from family goes against tradition.

The appearance of this Star is not a good omen. To maintain other people's support and friendship, try to be more open, outgoing and friendly.

Leopard's Tail

The Chinese consider leopards to be some of the fiercest animals in the jungle, who can cause a lot of trouble to those who happen to get in their way, or step on their tails.

If this Star appears in your horoscope it is best to be cautious, careful, discreet and maintain a low profile to avoid provoking anyone or arousing trouble.

Loose Hair

After the age of 20 Chinese noblemen and gentry would grow their hair long, wearing it tied up in a knot at the top of their heads. However, during periods of mourning for the death of a family member, they would let their hair fall down like a waterfall to show that they were too filled with sorrow to worry about personal appearance.

This Star is a bad omen. If it appears in your horoscope, remember to take care of younger family members, and keep an eye on safety at home.

Lunar Threat

The ancient Chinese believed that many malevolent spirits and entities spread misfortune and dangers among the populace. Among these, the Star Lunar Threat is one of the least serious, since it deals with traps and tricks posed by members of the opposite sex.

Should this Star appear in your horoscope, you need to be cautious regarding potential difficulties and unexpected problems in romantic relationships.

Lying Corpse

In ancient China, to die peacefully at home was considered to be a blessing. In contrast, to die in an accident in the street or some other public place was considered the worst thing that could happen. Such unexpected and 'poorly timed' deaths were considered to be a kind of divine retribution for a person's bad deeds.

When this Star appears, be very careful not to commit any wrong-doings, and at the same time pay special attention to safety when engaged in outdoor activities.

Official Spell

This is one of the five 'Magic Spell' Stars in the Chinese Horoscope. The ancient Chinese believed that the family would get entangled in lawsuits as a result of an encounter with this spell.

When this Star appears, people need to watch their conduct and follow the rules. They should be very careful in managing their affairs to avoid legal problems or lawsuits.

Pointing at the Back

Based on their long struggle for survival, the ancient Chinese realized that the most dangerous enemies were those behind one's back. Such people hid and wait for an opportunity to attack, either verbally or physically, without warning.

When this Star appears, people need to hide their weaknesses, and be aware of any hidden enemies or gossip around them.

Pool of Indulgence

One of China's most cruel and wicked emperors, Emperor Zhou of the Shang Dynasty, built a pool which he filled with wine inside his luxurious palace. He invited his royal followers and beautiful women to come and be merry by drinking or even swimming in the wine. This symbol of over-indulgence warns against bad habits and self-indulgent behaviour. If this Star appears in your horoscope, you need to avoid bad habits – if you don't, you will miss out on good opportunities and waste a great deal of money.

Six Harms

To the ancient Chinese peasants, floods, droughts, frosts, wars, plagues of locusts and other insects and so on were the major harms faced by their crops. The occurrence of any one of these harms would seriously damage their income. The appearance of the Star 'Six Harms' is a very bad omen to the economy of the people concerned.

When this Star appears within a Sign, watch out for the economic growth of your business, and for sudden changes such as a dramatic drop in sales and production or cancellation of contracts, etc.

Sudden Collapse

A building, project or business will ultimately collapse if it lacks a solid foundation – one which must be steadily maintained. 'Sudden Collapse', as its name suggests, is considered to be a bad omen. In order to prevent this kind of tragedy, people have to build up their foundation slowly but surely.

When this Star appears it is a warning to be very careful about business, especially concerning financial matters.

Sudden Death

Due to the inadequate knowledge of medicine in ancient China, a lot of sudden deaths were believed to be caused by the unpredictable will of the gods. This kind of ignorance kept many from trying to get medical care when they needed it.

This Star is one of the worst Unlucky Stars in the Chinese Horoscope. When this Star appears within your sign, keep all medical appointments and try to take preventative measures before it is too late.

Swallowed Up

The ancient Chinese peasants faced numerous threats to their possessions. Their grain might be swallowed up by birds, their poultry and domestic animals might be swallowed up by wolves and tigers, and, in their barns, their stored food might be swallowed up by rats or bandits.

When this Star appears, people have to take good care of their belongings and protect from other people what they have worked hard to earn.

Sword's Edge

Swords, as well as knives and other sharp weapons, were not favoured by the peace-loving ancient Chinese. They were considered too dangerous. Similarly, the 'Sword's Edge' Star is considered to be a bad omen, calling for precautionary measures regarding your personal safety. This is especially relevant when engaging in outdoor activities.

Threat of Disasters

The ancient Chinese believed that malevolent spirits brought different kinds of threats into people's daily lives. One of these was the 'Threat of Disasters', which as the name suggests brought disaster if people did not take measures to protect themselves beforehand.

The appearance of this Star is a serious warning. People should pay more attention to protecting their property and personal safety. Avoid risk-taking. 'Safety first' is the rule to follow.

Threat of Robbery

The ancient Chinese believed that different kinds of malevolent spirit went around creating problems for people. Based on this, the concept of several 'Threat Stars' developed in the Chinese Horoscope. This is one of them.

When this Star appears, people should be careful regarding their security and personal safety. Avoid walking alone at night, and make sure that all windows and doors are securely locked.

Tightened Loop

Loops were commonly used by the ancient Chinese to catch animals. Consequently, a loop is usually considered to be the symbol of a trap. A person, as well as an animal, might get caught or even strangled by a tightened loop. So it is better to stay away from any kind of loop, noose or rope.

The appearance of this Star is a warning signal. Keep your eyes wide open to watch out for the traps in front of you. Otherwise, it will prove very difficult to get out of the traps and dilemmas.

Tongues Wag

Confucianism endorses the adage 'Silence is Golden.' In ancient Chinese society, gossiping – especially rumour-mongering – was definitely looked down upon.

Should this Star appear in your horoscope it is a warning to you to refrain from gossip. Wagging tongues will not only hurt others, but you as well.

Watch-dog of the Year

In Chinese mythology, a very fierce animal called 'Year' went about swallowing people just as a New Year was ushered in. To protect themselves the ancient Chinese used firecrackers to scare it away. Over time, this fierce animal would be tamed and became the Watch-dog of the Year among the Chinese folk. Still, it could be quite dangerous if irritated.

When this Star appears, it is best to behave, keep a low profile and take care not to offend anyone. To avoid problems, keep in mind the phrase 'let sleeping dogs lie'.

White Tiger

In ancient China, it was the tiger and not the lion who was considered king of the jungle. The white tiger was the most fierce and feared of all tigers, and gradually became a symbol of violence and danger.

When this Star appears, people need to stay alert for danger and sudden attacks, which could turn them into helpless victims.

Yearly Threat

The ancient Chinese believed that malevolent spirits brought dangers and problems into their daily lives. The Star 'Yearly Threat' was one of these. Its appearance is a bad omen.

When this Star appears, people need to improve relations with others, especially with lovers and spouses, to avoid endless arguments and quarrels.

Yellow Funeral Flag

In ancient times, the Chinese believed that the spirits of the newly dead floated aimlessly in the sky. To guide the spirits back home, their families would fly a yellow flag from the rooftop to signal where they lived. Not surprisingly, yellow flags soon became the symbol for death and funerals.

When this Star appears, people need to be extra careful about the health and safety of younger family members. Keep in mind that 'prevention is better than cure'.

Using Feng Shui to Improve Fortune:

Direction, Colours, Numbers and Lucky Charms

The ancient Chinese used the traditional Horoscope to predict their fortune on a yearly basis – they used the art of Feng Shui to improve their luck.

It was their belief that the application of tactical Feng Shui would change their bad luck into good, and make their good luck improve even more.

This same method is still effective in today's modern world.

There are four main elements which I will use in tactical Feng Shui:

◆ Directions
◆ Colours
◆ Numbers
◆ Lucky Charms

For each Sign, the significance and use of these four elements is as follows:

Directions

You should sleep or sit facing the directions indicated if you wish to improve your fortune.

To make this procedure very simple, divide your house or room into nine imaginary squares (see figures for individual Signs, below). Then, using a compass, check the exact direction of each square. This will help to ensure that you do not make a mistake with the direction.

You should sit in the relevant directions at work or while studying; this will ensure that your achievements are much better than the Stars intended. To improve health and achieve a good night's sleep, position the headboard of your bed towards the favourable directions.

Colours

According to Chinese tradition, each of the five elements has its own representative colour. Fire is represented by red, purple and pink, Earth by yellow and brown, and so on. As your Feng Shui master I will suggest specific colours for each Sign to improve your fortune.

Use these colours in paints, wall coverings, rugs, drapes and curtains. This will be sure to bring you good fortune.

Numbers

Use the lucky numbers indicated for your Sign wherever possible; they will bring you good fortune in the year ahead.

Lucky Charms

Feng Shui Masters believe that special objects can be used as a medium between human beings and nature. The fortune of the recipient is greatly improved, as the positive wave of energy from nature is passed through the object or 'lucky charm' on to the recipient.

Each Sign is allocated its own 'lucky charm' depending on the object best suited to the sign. These 'lucky charms' change yearly.

The Chinese have long believed in the power of crystals. Carrying with you a small crystal figurine of your lucky charm will increase your good fortune. Jade is also considered a powerful stone. Figures crafted in crystal or jade can be purchased at traditional Chinese shops.

The Mouse

As seen in the chapter for the Mouse, those born under this Sign will have a pretty good year because of the appearance of several 'Lucky Stars' within the Sign. In order to make your career and business more successful, I suggest applying the following tactical Feng Shui.

N. West		N. East
West		East
S. West	South	

North

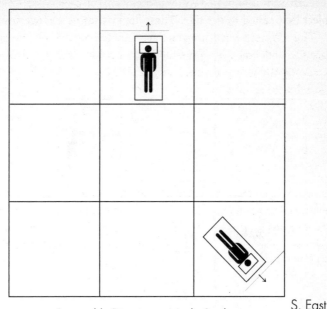

S. East

Favourable Directions   North, Southeast
Favourable Colours   Yellow, Brown
Lucky Numbers   1, 8, 10, 17, 19, 26, 28, 35, 37, 44
Lucky Charms   Peach and Guava

The Ox

It is perfectly clear from the chapter for the Ox that those born under this Sign are in for a rough year. However, the psychology of the exercise is to get the attitude right – the Horoscope is simply a warning system. The preventative measures already suggested will ensure that there is not much to worry about, and if the following Feng Shui tactics are followed there will be nothing to worry about. In order to help activate additional protective energy, I suggest applying the following tactical Feng Shui.

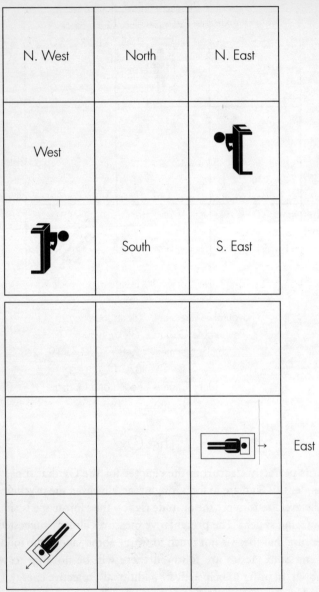

N. West	North	N. East
West		
	South	S. East

S. West

Favourable Directions East, Southwest
Favourable Colours Blue, Grey, Black
Lucky Numbers 2, 5, 11, 14, 20, 22, 29, 32, 38, 41
Lucky Charm The Kirin

The Tiger

As mentioned in the chapter for the Tiger, those born under this Sign can expect to have a rough year due to the appearance of two Unlucky Stars and the absence of any Lucky Stars. Tigers can equip themselves to weather the storm by taking some preventative measures in advance. They should not worry unduly. If they use the following Feng Shui tactics they should have nothing to worry about. In order to help activate additional protective energy, I suggest applying the following tactical Feng Shui.

N. West		N. East
West		East
S. West		S. East

North

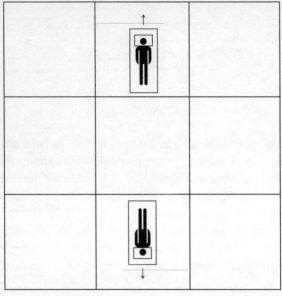

South

Favourable Directions South, North
Favourable Colours White, Blue
Lucky Numbers 3, 7, 12, 16, 21, 25, 30, 34, 39, 43
Lucky Charm Buddha's Fingers

The Rabbit

As seen in the chapter for the Rabbit, those born under this Sign will have a very busy and productive year. They should take care of their health, and be alert to personal safety. I recommend the following Feng Shui tactics to help prevent ill health and keep the Rabbit more secure. In order to help activate achievement in education and business, improvement in health and sound sleeping patterns, I suggest applying the following tactical Feng Shui.

	North	N. East
West		
S. West	South	S. East

N. West

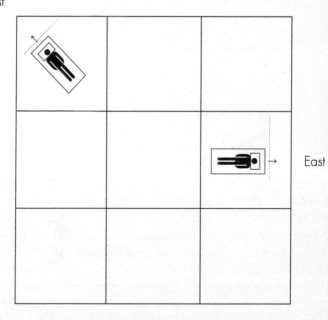

East

Favourable Directions	East, Northwest
Favourable Colours	Red, Pink, Purple
Lucky Numbers	2, 9, 11, 18, 20, 27, 29, 36, 38, 45
Lucky Charm	A Pair of Carps

The Dragon

As seen in the chapter for the Dragon, 1999 will be a very active and energetic year for those born under this Sign. This is a new year for them to develop new projects with quite successful results. However, if they wish to be even more successful they should apply the following tactical Feng Shui. In order to help activate increased good fortune and assist new project development, I suggest applying the following tactical Feng Shui.

N. West	North	N. East
		East
S. West	South	

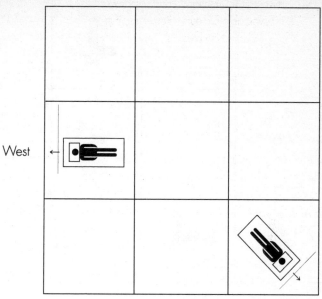

West

S. East

Favourable Directions West, Southeast
Favourable Colours Green, Beige
Lucky Numbers 4, 6, 13, 15, 22, 24, 31, 33,
40, 42
Lucky Charm Deer

The Snake

As seen in the chapter for the Snake, 1999 will be a rather tedious and sluggish year for those born under this Sign. Their careers or business ventures could be destroyed unless they take some preventative measures as discussed in the monthly predictions. In addition, if they wish to have a prosperous year, they would be wise to follow these Feng Shui tactics. In order to help activate preventative measures against a dull, sluggish year, I suggest applying the following tactical Feng Shui.

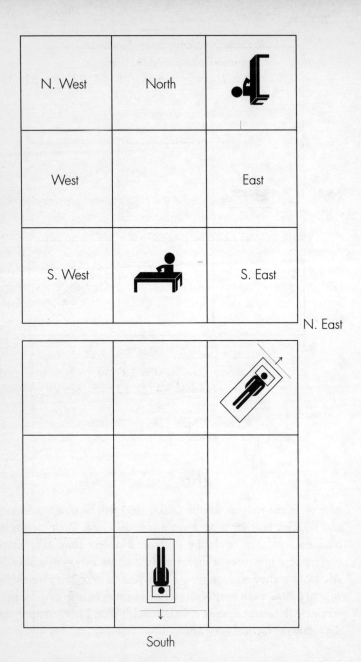

N. West	North	
West		East
S. West		S. East

N. East

South

The Horse

As mentioned in the chapter for the Horse, those born under this Sign will have to struggle very hard in business this year. But this will also be a romantic year for them. However, if they want to strengthen their business development and find a suitable lover, the Horse should apply the following Feng Shui tactics during 1999. In order to help strengthen business success and enhance the opportunities for a healthy romance, I suggest applying the following tactical Feng Shui.

N. West		N. East
West		East
S. West	South	

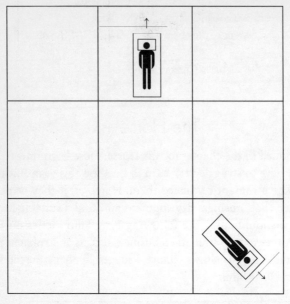

S. East

Favourable Directions	North, Southeast
Favourable Colours	Blue, Grey
Lucky Numbers	4, 9, 13, 18, 22, 27, 31, 36, 40, 45
Lucky Charm	Jade Ruyi-sceptre

The Sheep

As mentioned in the chapter for the Sheep, those born under this Sign will have a fortunate year in 1999 because of the appearance of several Lucky Stars within their Sign. However, if they want to make the year more joyful and successful, they should apply the following tactics. In order to help activate greater joy and success, I suggest applying the following tactical Feng Shui.

N. West		N. East
West		East
	South	S. East

North

S. West

Favourable Directions Southwest, North
Favourable Colours Yellow, Brown
Lucky Numbers 1, 5, 10, 14, 19, 23, 28, 32, 37, 41
Lucky Charm Flying Horse

The Monkey

As mentioned in the chapter for the Monkey, those born under this Sign have problems financially and physically in 1999. Fortunately, the two Lucky Stars that appear within the Sign should help them to solve their problems. However, if they want to have a peaceful year without any threats, they should apply the following Feng Shui tactics. In order to help activate greater peace and tranquillity, I suggest applying the following tactical Feng Shui.

N. West		N. East
West		East
	South	S. East

North

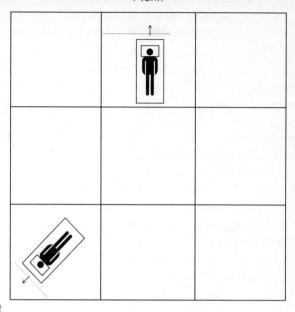

S. West

Favourable Directions   North, Southwest
Favourable Colours   White, Black
Lucky Numbers   2, 6, 11, 15, 20, 24, 29, 33,
                     38, 42
Lucky Charm   Turtle's Shell

The Rooster

As indicated in the chapter for the Rooster, those born under this Sign will have a very exciting year. Their finances and their careers will be up and down like a roller coaster, however. For a peaceful and stable year they should apply the following tactical Feng Shui to improve their good luck. In order to help activate greater stability and harmony, I suggest applying the following tactical Feng Shui.

N. West	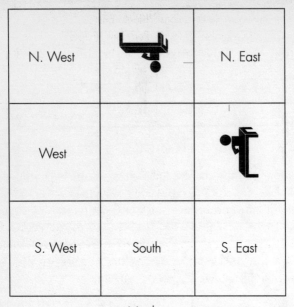	N. East
West		
S. West	South	S. East

North

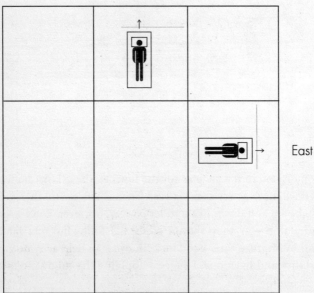

East

Favourable Directions   North, East
Favourable Colours   Red, Pink, Purple
Lucky Numbers   3, 8, 12, 17, 21, 26, 30, 35, 39, 44
Lucky Charms   Dragon and Phoenix

The Dog

As mentioned in the chapter for the Dog, those born under this Sign will have a pretty successful and productive year in 1999. But they should not show off too much in order to prevent a sudden collapse. However, if they want to keep their handsome rewards after long struggling, they should apply the following Feng Shui tactics. In order to help activate increased financial rewards, I suggest applying the following tactical Feng Shui.

	North	N. East
West		East
S. West		S. East

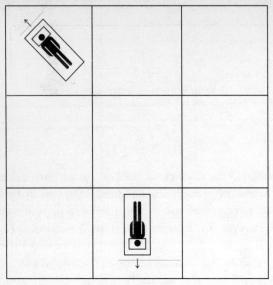

South

Favourable Directions South, Northwest
Favourable Colours White, Green
Lucky Numbers 5, 9, 14, 18, 23, 27, 32, 36, 41, 45
Lucky Charm Jade Rabbit

The Pig

As mentioned in the chapter for the Pig, those born under this Sign will have a very rough year because the appearance of several Unlucky Stars within their Sign. However, if they can equip themselves psychologically and take some preventative measures accordingly in advance, they should not worry too much about that. If they use the following Feng Shui tactics as additional protection, then they should have nothing to worry about. In order to help activate additional protective energy, I suggest applying the following tactical Feng Shui.

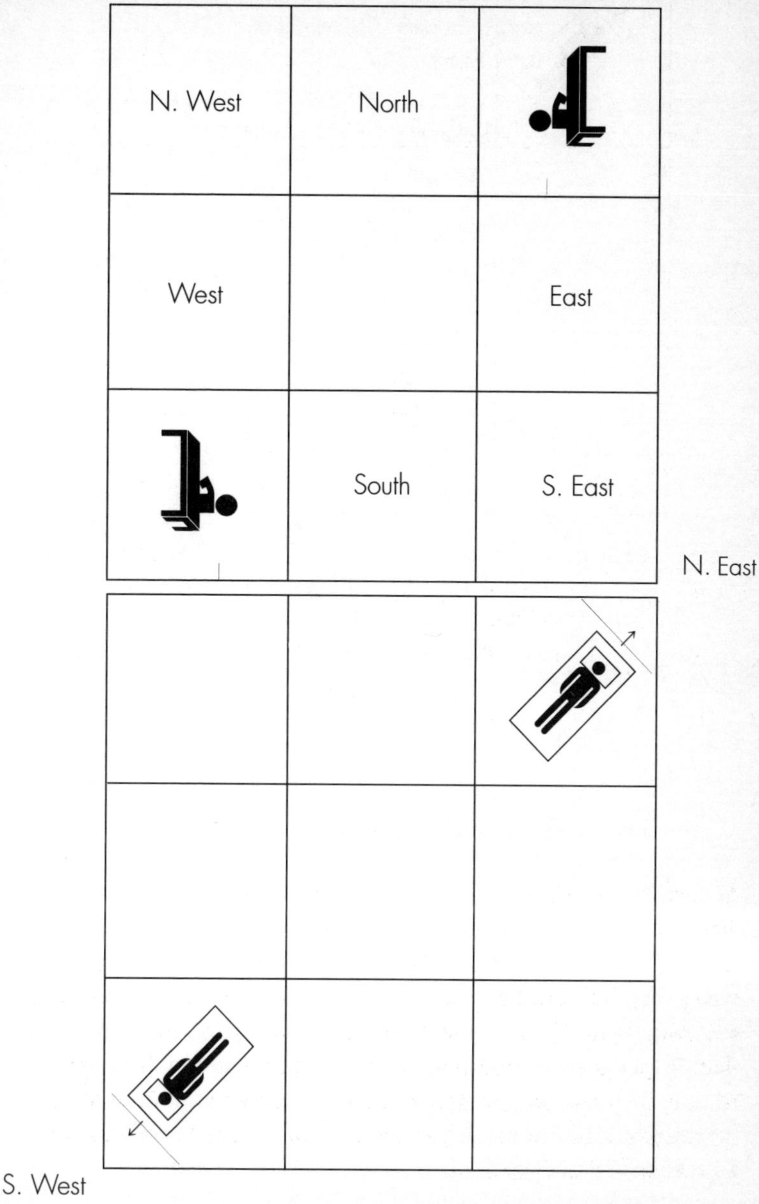
N. West
North
West
East
South
S. East
N. East
S. West

Favourable Directions	Northeast, Southwest
Favourable Colours	Yellow, Black
Lucky Numbers	4, 7, 13, 16, 22, 25, 31, 34, 40, 43
Lucky Charm	A Pair of Sheep